D0970499

UNDERCOVER BOSS

UNDERCOVER BOSS

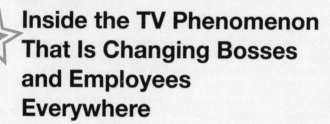

Inside the TV Phenomenon That Is Changing Bosses and Employees Everywhere

Stephen Lambert and Eli Holzman

with Mark Levine

JOSSEY-BASS
A Wiley Imprint
www.josseybass.com

Published by Jossey-Bass
A Wiley Imprint
989 Market Street, San Francisco, CA 94103-1741—www.josseybass.com

Readers should be aware that Internet Web sites offered as citations and/or sources for further information may have changed or disappeared between the time this was written and when it is read.

Limit of Liability/Disclaimer of Warranty: While the publisher and author have used their best efforts in preparing this book, they make no representations or warranties with respect to the accuracy or completeness of the contents of this book and specifically disclaim any implied warranties of merchantability or fitness for a particular purpose. No warranty may be created or extended by sales representatives or written sales materials. The advice and strategies contained herein may not be suitable for your situation. You should consult with a professional where appropriate. Neither the publisher nor author shall be liable for any loss of profit or any other commercial damages, including but not limited to special, incidental, consequential, or other damages.

Jossey-Bass books and products are available through most bookstores. To contact Jossey-Bass directly call our Customer Care Department within the U.S. at 800-956-7739, outside the U.S. at 317-572-3986, or fax 317-572-4002.

Jossey-Bass also publishes its books in a variety of electronic formats. Some content that appears in print may not be available in electronic books.

Library of Congress Cataloging-in-Publication Data
Lambert, Stephen.
  Undercover boss : inside the TV phenomenon that is changing bosses and employees everywhere / Stephen Lambert, Eli Holzman.
    p. cm.
  ISBN 978-0-470-91600-1 (hardback); ISBN 978-0-470-93982-6 (ebk);
  ISBN 978-0-470-93983-3 (ebk); ISBN 978-0-470-93984-0 (ebk)
  1. Supervision of employees—United States. 2. Supervisors—United States. 3. Management—United States. 4. Reality television programs—United States. I. Holzman, Eli. II. Title.
  HF5549.12.L35 2010
  658.3'02—dc22
                                                          2010039870

Printed in the United States of America
FIRST EDITION
HB Printing   10 9 8 7 6 5 4 3 2 1

For Ron Scalera
1960–2010

 **CONTENTS**

UNDERCOVER BOSS

# INTRODUCTION

The pitch for *Undercover Boss* was our first as Studio Lambert. We had come together a few weeks earlier to form a new television production company in the United States. Six months before that, Stephen had launched the business in the United Kingdom. It was late 2008, just as the recession had hit and television advertising revenues had collapsed, but despite the tough economic times, we were optimistic. Now, after all the dreamy talk around the kitchen table in Eli's Venice Beach apartment, we were finally going out to sell a show. Or at least try to.

The broadcast and cable network buyers in Los Angeles hear dozens of pitches every day. The overwhelming majority are rejected—not to your face, but in the after-pitch feedback to your agent. They are the smart ones wearing ties and dark suits who patiently attend all pitches and then try to hustle a deal afterwards. Usually this means listening to endless euphemisms for *no:* "We like the idea, but we just don't think it will connect with our demo." "We tried that kind of idea recently, but the focus group numbers killed it." "We're looking for something bigger, noisier, more special." To have any chance of making a sale, you have to fall in love with your idea. You then have to convey that love with every fiber of your body. Then you need to have a thick skin. And luck.

The idea for our show started in the United Kingdom in 2008, when British Airways opened its new $6 billion terminal at Heathrow. It was a disaster. Thousands of families heading on vacation faced chaos after the prestigious terminal was reduced to a shambles on its opening day by the complete failure of its baggage system. The beleaguered chief executive of BA, Willie Walsh, was hounded by news reporters. Someone from the *Times* asked, "'When was the last time he travelled as a punter [paying customer],' exposing himself to the kind of service that led one angry passenger on the day that T5 opened to remark: 'People like us that are treated like cattle, as usual, by British Airways'? 'As a punter on BA?' said Walsh. 'I can't because people in BA recognise me.'"

We wondered whether that was true. Would ordinary workers in large corporations recognize their big boss if he or she were dressed like them and they were told that here was a new trainee trying out their kind of job? We suspected they wouldn't. Fortunately, Britain's Channel 4 agreed, and ordered a pilot that would let us test our theory.

We shot the UK pilot in the late summer of 2008 with the boss of a budget vacation resort company. It worked. The boss wasn't recognized. He learned a great deal about what was wrong with his business. When he eventually told his fellow workers who he really was, he decided to reward them with promotions and training courses. It was a very emotional ending to his time undercover. We didn't wait to finish editing the British pilot before pitching our show in the United States. We now had the most valuable thing anyone who wants to sell an idea to American TV networks can possibly have—tape.

Being able to visualize one's idea for a TV show is a huge advantage in the ultracompetitive program selling game. With so much at stake, buyers find it hard to take a risk on formats that are just "paper" ideas. The reason television producers with a British connection have made so many reality hits in the United States in the last decade is that they can sell their paper ideas to British networks (who, for various reasons, mainly to do with the way the business is regulated, are less risk averse) and then use the tape of the British show to sell the idea to America. It was the business model on which we had based our new company.

We spent days in an edit suite preparing what in TV land is called a "sizzle reel"—a five-minute sales tape. Our sizzle was good because we could use the best bits from the pilot we had just shot in Britain. "In these difficult times," declared the opening captions, which we put next to sweeping aerials of gleaming skyscrapers and shots of stock price ticker boards with all the numbers in bright red, "even the most successful companies are struggling. In the boardroom, it's all too easy to lose touch. The bosses know their profits and their losses, but do they know what's happening on the front line?"

The notion that the super-executives who run America's biggest companies might give up their expense accounts and chauffeur-driven limos to work incognito alongside their workers was audacious. Corporate heavyweights of the kind we envisaged have every minute of their schedules planned out weeks, more like months, in advance. We'd be asking them to clear a week or more to take part in our program. Yet appearing in a reality show would be the last thing they would think was a sensible use of their precious time. But love is blind. We were smitten, and all we cared about was selling our show. How we actually made it was tomorrow's problem.

The week we took our sizzle around town was special— not just for our fledgling company, but for America. It was the first week of November 2008, and the country was in the process of electing a new president. When the result was declared, Democrat-supporting Hollywood went wild. We hoped the euphoria would help our chances of selling our show. Certainly everyone was thinking about the state of the economy and how the new administration could improve it. There was widespread disillusionment with the leaders of corporate America, but here we were proposing a TV show that would put them center stage as heroes on a mission to learn, improve their business, and thank their employees. It was either genius timing, or we were way out of keeping with the zeitgeist.

The networks seemed to like our sizzle reel, but it's often hard to tell what they really think. When you are pitching a show around town, each buyer knows that when you leave his or her office you are going up the road to offer the same idea to their competitor. If buyers give you meaningful feedback at this stage, their comments might end up improving an idea that will air on a rival network. So most of them keep their counsel, but a few did tell us a little of what they thought. For some, the notion of the boss as a "fish out of water" was appealing. They wanted to see a well-to-do person struggling in the real world and wanted to focus on whether they could live like an ordinary Joe. Others thought the prospect of poorly performing employees being fired was what would make the show work. But this wasn't what we had in mind. We wanted something that celebrated the unsung heroes of the companies and showed the boss making systemic improvements.

When, in the middle of the week, we went to pitch the show to CBS, our expectations were low. This was, and still is, America's #1 network. It has a hugely successful slate of dramas like *CSI: Crime Scene Investigation, NCIS,* and *The Mentalist* and popular comedies such as *Two and a Half Men* and *The Big Bang Theory.* With such a strong collection of scripted shows, CBS hadn't found room for many reality shows. But the three it did have were monsters: *Survivor, Amazing Race,* and *Big Brother* all had many years of ratings success. All three of them were "serial elimination shows" that built viewer loyalty as the audiences came to know the cast over many episodes, rooting for the contestants they thought should ultimately win. We were proposing something completely different. Our show had closed-end episodes with a different cast each week; it was set in real workplaces, not exotic locations; and there wasn't a huge prize at the end of the season. Selling it here was a long shot.

The new head of reality television at CBS, Jen Bresnan, was far away in a jungle somewhere overseeing the latest series of *Survivor,* so our pitch was going to be to her boss, the president of CBS Entertainment, Nina Tassler. Born to a Puerto Rican mother and a Jewish father, Nina is not a tall woman, but she's a giant in network television. She was the person who had bought *CSI* and turned it into the world's most successful drama series. She had worked closely with Leslie Moonves, the all-powerful chief executive of CBS, for nearly two decades. We doubted that, with such a distinguished record in scripted programming, Nina would have much time or interest in a new reality show.

After a few minutes telling her about our new company and explaining the premise of the show, we offered to play the reel. Nina pressed a button and an enormous plasma screen swung out from the wall so that we could all watch while sitting on her plush sofas. By now we had seen the reel a dozen times, so while we watched quietly we also tried to sneak glances to see how Nina was reacting. We couldn't be sure, but it looked as though she was dabbing away a tear as the reel ended. We waited for her to respond.

When she did, she focused on the emotion of the show. She talked about the importance of recognizing and celebrating the hardworking people who make businesses run. She loved the idea that we would bring them to the attention of the boss in a way that allowed the discovery to be genuine. She immediately saw that the show didn't need a big cash prize to have network appeal. And Nina recognized that seeing the Big Guy struggling to do Average Joe's job offered a great deal of comedic potential.

As we emerged into the sunshine outside CBS's Studio City offices, we turned to our agent, Greg Lipstone, from ICM. "That was about as good a pitch meeting as it's possible to have," we said. Greg smiled and immediately placed a call in to Nina to see whether she felt the same. "We want to go straight to pilot and pay for casting the bosses of an initial series of six episodes," was the answer that came back. Although some of the other buyers also said they wanted to do a deal, it was an easy decision to go with CBS.

There was just one problem: CBS wanted our pilot in time for the "Upfronts." These are the massive schedule-unveiling events that each broadcast network holds during one week in mid-May in New York City. In grand venues like Carnegie

Hall or Lincoln Center, advertisers are shown clips from next season's schedule, and in the weeks afterward, they spend billions of dollars buying advertising slots in these new schedules. Network television works on an extraordinarily choreographed annual cycle that culminates in Upfront Week. All the scripted show pilots have to be delivered to networks in late April so that a decision can be taken in the few weeks leading up to the announcements about which shows live or die. Those that get picked up have to be ready to go on-air in September with runs of 13 episodes that then might be extended to a full-season run of 22 episodes or more. The fact that the *Undercover Boss* pilot would be considered as part of this process meant that we knew from the start there was a chance we could end up on the main schedule that runs from September to May, rather than just be another of the summer reality shows, which often come and go.

With the winter holidays fast approaching, we had very little time. We had to find a boss who was willing to go undercover by March at the very latest, so that we'd have enough time to edit the pilot. We also had to find five other bosses willing to do the show so that CBS would feel confident we could actually produce a series if they decided to order it. In the United Kingdom it had taken 11 weeks to find one company for the pilot. We had barely that much time to find six. We considered telling CBS we couldn't manage it. In the end, we decided we had to go for it. We hired the best people we knew, starting with Stef Wagstaffe, a talented show runner known to Stephen for her work overseeing one of the other series he had created, *Wife Swap,* on ABC. Almost immediately, a small army went to work reaching out to every large company in America.

Usually our team didn't make it past the first call. Companies struggling to deal with the economic crisis had no time to spare. Auto manufacturers and others in the process of accepting TARP funds turned us down immediately. The team's confidence began to wane, but every now and then some companies responded favorably. A few executives were genuinely intrigued by the opportunity to see their operations firsthand and to do it anonymously. That, however, was just the beginning of the process.

There was still the small matter of the participation agreement that CBS required the companies to sign. It ran to more than a dozen pages and was based on the kind of contract that was standard for contestants in big-prize elimination shows where there is no shortage of people wanting to take part. The well-heeled lawyers at the large corporations we were now talking to had never seen anything like it. This wasn't going to be easy. We needed to have free access to each company's facilities; we needed the freedom to film without interruption; and, most crucially, the company had to accept that it would have no editorial control and would not be permitted to see its episode until it aired. On top of all of that, we needed more than a week of the boss's time to film, an eternity in the context of their packed schedules. And with only a pilot order, we couldn't even promise them that the episode would air. Our challenge was further compounded by CBS's high standards—Jen Bresnan kept reminding us that we needed huge companies with several kinds of visually interesting frontline jobs and highly charismatic bosses.

But things did start moving forward with one company. And it was a good one. In a show where the boss has to get his hands dirty, what could be better than America's largest waste management business? At the Houston headquarters of the $12 billion Waste Management Corporation, we had a champion. Her name was Lynn Brown, and she was responsible for corporate PR. She thought that what we were offering was madly risky, but she also thought it might just be the PR coup of her career if it all went well. All she had to do was convince her boss that being on a network reality show wasn't going to be career suicide.

Lawrence O'Donnell III was an engineer and lawyer by training. He joined Waste Management in 2000 as senior vice president, general counsel, and corporate secretary, and four years later he was promoted to president and chief operating officer. Larry was responsible for the company's 43,000 employees, and he believed in spending time with them. He frequently went out into his field operations, but knew that he was always treated like the president of the company. When Lynn suggested that he work with them anonymously while taking part in our television show, Larry could see that he might learn something new. But he had no desire to be on television.

Fortunately, Lynn didn't give up. Eventually she convinced Larry that he should at least talk to the program makers. Eli called him in Houston and used all his charm to persuade Larry that the upside for Waste Management was considerable, and the downside . . . well, don't worry about the downside because it wasn't going to happen. Eli began his career working as assistant to the legendary film producer Harvey Weinstein. The master taught him how to be persuasive. Larry began to waver.

Two other people finally convinced Larry to do the show. The first was Stephen Martin, the chief executive of a British engineering firm, who had been filmed for the second episode in the United Kingdom, as by this point Channel 4 had ordered a series. Stephen was the first of what was to become a growing and passionate group of *Undercover Boss* alumni—chief executives who after doing the show were evangelical about the experience. He was more than happy to tell Larry about his dealings with Studio Lambert and why he thought it was something any boss should do. Larry called him several times.

The other person was Larry's wife, Dare. True to her name, Dare told Larry that he should take the risk. "He's a cautious man," she later told us. "I told him it was time to be a little bit reckless." Larry decided to leap into the unknown. Lynn rang to say that he was willing to sign our contract. We booked a crew, shot an interview with Larry, and submitted him and Waste Management to CBS. A few days later, Jen informed us that our pilot casting was approved. We now had a show to make.

The next few weeks were a whirlwind of activity. While preparing to film with Waste Management, we visited bosses and companies across the country searching for the other five companies. The Ingram family, owners of White Castle, the fast-food chain featuring steam-grilled burgers, welcomed us with open arms at their Ohio headquarters; Bill Carstanjen, COO of Churchill Downs, owners of America's biggest horse racing tracks, agreed to saddle up; and Coby Brooks, CEO of Hooters of America, thought he could learn much by working in his restaurants with his mainly female staff.

Filming the pilot was an adventure. Waste Management's operations stretch across the country and, to give Larry a good sample of various frontline jobs, we had an ambitious schedule that took us through three states and nine cities. Larry was sure he would be recognized in Houston, where he was based. He told us he had met Gilbert, his shift supervisor for Port-O-Let cleaning, on several occasions and that Gilbert was bound to bust him. We decided to gamble and sent Larry to see Gilbert anyway. Much to Larry's surprise—with some stubble on his chin and a pair of coveralls as his disguise—he pulled off his undercover mission without a hitch. Gilbert looked him right in the face, told him he'd be cleaning toilets, and sent him to work. Gilbert didn't recognize Larry despite checking on him throughout the day. Larry worked a hard, long shift, got to know an inspiring employee named Fred, and experienced his own productivity targets firsthand. It was just what Larry had signed up for.

The story of the first episode is told in detail in the first chapter of this book. Needless to say, Larry learned a lot. We learned a lot. And by the time we finished the shoot, we were exhausted but utterly exhilarated. After the crew had packed away their gear, Eli sent this e-mail to Stephen in London.

Sent: 31 March 2009 23:59

Subject: That's a wrap

We've just wrapped.

With garbage trucks arrayed, the stage, jib and staff in place—running late of course—and finally ready to roll on our finale . . . massive gray clouds rolled in, thunder clapped . . . and it began to rain. We scrambled for cover. The senior staff from Waste Management grumbled a bit and moved back inside. Larry climbed into the cab of a truck to save his suit. Stef and I dragged tarps over scary electrical stuff.

And we paused watching big Florida rain drops hitting the pavement . . . and wondered (for not the first time) whether our decision to lavish our hard-fought and much-needed money on this finale (which now seemed a total waste) was a ruinous one.

Seeing the looks on our faces, Stef [our show runner] said, "don't worry, it'll stop raining."

And a moment later, it did.

The clouds cleared. It got bright. 100 staffers filled the lot. Our stars moved to the front of the crowd. Larry took the stage. And we played terrific clips from our 10 day adventure, celebrating Waste Management's previously unsung heroes. They beamed, some cried. Everyone laughed and cheered. The jib moved beautifully. The helicopter circled and hovered. And we just wrapped one hell of an episode.

Chris Carlson [the executive on-site from CBS] was thrilled. He assured us Nina will love it.

Larry felt his experience was such a good one, he volunteered to call other CEOs who are considering participating.

We are all going to get very drunk now. And tomorrow we'll dive back into casting, roll up our sleeves for editing. And generally get on with it.

In the month that followed, we scrambled to edit the pilot. Typically this would take seven or eight weeks. We had only four. We knew we had great material, so we were all motivated to cut the show together quickly and well. Jen and her two colleagues, Chris Castallo and Chris Carlson, continued to push us at every point to make the pilot as good as possible. We really need to understand Larry's motivation when he does each of these undercover jobs, they insisted. And we need to show more clearly how stressful Larry is finding these jobs. And the music needs to be better in all these places. These and many other notes helped greatly. As did the huge muffin basket they sent the whole staff as we struggled to meet the deadlines.

With Larry's help, and footage from his episode to show, Joe DePinto from 7-Eleven came aboard, along with Joel Manby from Herschend Family Entertainment. We now knew we could make a first series with some seriously well-known brands.

We turned in the pilot and the names of the additional companies to CBS just before Upfronts. CBS tests its pilots to large groups of viewers in screening rooms in Las Vegas. When the test results of our pilot came back, the numbers were good—too good. These can't be right, said some high-ups at CBS; test it again. They did and got the same result. A few days before the network television and the advertising community came together for their annual powwow, Jen called. "This is your official pickup call. We are ordering *Undercover Boss* as a midseason show. We'll need it to be ready to air by the end of the year. Congratulations. We're all very excited."

The following week, we sat in Carnegie Hall as a couple of thousand media buyers and advertising executives watched clips from our pilot. To us it seemed that our clips got more laughs and more applause than any other new show. But we were proud parents; we knew we were hardly neutral judges. But then we listened to the chatter at the party after the presentation and on the blog sites. Everyone agreed we'd made a big impact. Larry, Dare, and Lynn were there too. "You're going to be a star," said a group of CBS's most well-known actors. Larry looked bemused.

Over the summer and fall months, we worked hard to shoot five more undercover missions. Then CBS extended the order, and we were able to sign up wunderkind founder CEO Michael Rubin and his e-commerce juggernaut, GSI Commerce; Rick Arquilla, boss of American perennial Roto-Rooter; and brothers

Jim and Chris McCann, owners of 1-800-Flowers.com. As the episodes emerged from the edit suite, everything we hoped for the series seemed to be coming true. The show delivered comedy and emotion. Our bosses learned that sometimes what made sense sitting in corporate HQ was gobbledygook when experienced in the trenches. And they discovered that they employed some truly impressive people who frequently went well beyond the call of duty.

As the weeks and months went by, we felt increasingly confident that we had a very strong series, but we still had no idea when it would actually see the light of day. We heard that the CBS schedulers might want to show it in December. That was okay, but a little disappointing. It's hard to make an impact so close to the holiday period. We pressed on, casting, shooting, and editing at all hours.

But December came, and we still had no news on an air date. Then, a few days before the holidays, Jen called. "I've got some news. We have an air date for the premiere of the show. It's quite a special slot. We're going to launch *Undercover Boss* in the post–Super Bowl slot." Christmas had come early. It was an extraordinary present. The Superbowl is the most popular television event of the year. Any show that plays immediately after it is guaranteed a huge audience, or at least is guaranteed a huge audience at the start of the show. Whether we could hold that audience would be the big question.

On a sunny evening, February 7, 2010, we went to the Sun Life Stadium in Miami Gardens to see Super Bowl XLIV. Eli invited his father, and Stephen brought his 18-year-old son from London. We watched the game, but what was running through our minds was rather different from the thoughts of all the other fans. We were less worried about who won; we just wanted the game to be close so that the TV audience would stay watching until the end. But we didn't want it to be so close that the game went into extra time, delaying the start of our show, as we feared that would mean the audience would be too exhausted to stay up and watch it.

It was a close game. The New Orleans Saints came back from behind and in the middle of the fourth quarter went 24–17 ahead. But the Indianapolis Colts now had possession. If they got a touchdown in the next drive, the score would level. Extra time loomed. Then, out of the blue, Tracy Porter intercepted a pass by Peyton Manning and made a 74-yard takeaway run. His touchdown sealed the game for the Saints. The crowd went berserk. A nail-biting Super Bowl was over. But who would stay to watch a new reality show about a guy cleaning toilets?

Next morning we found out. The initial audience data came through slowly, without any detail. "We don't have the exact numbers yet, but we know it's going to be big," said CBS's ratings guru. Then Jen called. "We've got more data. We can't believe the retention numbers for *Undercover Boss*. After the first 10 minutes, everyone who was watching the show stayed until the end."

The 2010 Super Bowl was watched by 106 million people, the largest audience in American television history. By the time the half-hour postgame analysis show was over, that audience had dropped to 45 million. In the first 10 minutes of our show, that number fell to 37 million. But then it stayed level for the next 50 minutes. America was clearly captivated by its newest reality show. The official figure for our first season premiere was 38.6 million. It was the largest audience ever for the premiere of a reality show, the most watched new series premiere on television since *Dolly* in September 1987, and the third-largest post–Super Bowl audience for any show. We were stunned. CBS was pleased. Lynn was delighted. The gamble she had pushed Larry to take had paid off beyond her wildest dreams.

The following week, the show moved to its regular 9 P.M. Sunday slot, and the Hooters episode showed what we could do without a Super Bowl lead-in. More than 15 million people tuned in, despite huge numbers watching the Winter Olympics on NBC. By the time our first season was over, we knew that we had a copper-bottomed hit. With an average audience of more than 17 million, *Undercover Boss* was the most popular new show of the 2009–2010 television season. In these tough economic times, the show was clearly touching a nerve and resonating with its audience.

In an end-of-season review, Alessandra Stanley, chief television critic of the *New York Times,* examined the success of the show and concluded that "it's the humility of the workers, their genuine astonishment and thankfulness over small acts of benevolence, that is most striking. If nothing else, *Undercover Boss* is a reminder that in bad times, people are less eager to confront or provoke authority; mostly they wish for small favors and the big, serendipitous strokes of luck."

There was little question that CBS would commission a second season. Many wonder how we will still be able to pull off the conceit of the show now that it's so popular. Tune in to find out. We hope you will be moved and entertained.

Thank you for reading and for watching.

September 2010   Stephen & Eli
Culver City, California

SORTING THROUGH THE GARBAGE

"I don't know if it's because of The Sopranos, but some of the public thinks everyone in our industry is connected to the mob and that our frontline folks are ex-cons. I hoped going undercover would correct those mistaken notions."

Larry O'Donnell
COO, Waste Management

Randy Lawrence
Unemployed Construction Worker

How We Found the Boss

The bosses of large companies are not the kind of people who apply to be in reality TV shows. When we approached Waste Management, there was some trepidation, to say the least. "When Lynn [head of corporate PR] first brought this opportunity to me," said Larry O'Donnell after the show first aired [on BNET. com], "I told her she was absolutely crazy. There is no way I'm doing reality television. But the more we talked about it, well, we'd been working really hard for the last several years on our employee engagement, getting people engaged at every level of the company and opening up communication. We do employee surveys and, as we talked about it, this seemed like a very unique opportunity to drive that engagement."

In the end, Larry O'Donnell wasn't satisfied until we spoke to him personally and explained that unlike any other TV program where bosses of big companies let cameras into their businesses, he would be present in every scene. If he saw something he didn't like, he could then be seen on camera fixing whatever it was.

THE BOSS

Lawrence (Larry) O'Donnell III, president and COO.

HIS COVER

Randy Lawrence, an unemployed construction worker who's the subject of a documentary on entry-level jobs.

HIS COMPANY

Waste Management, Inc., is the leading provider of comprehensive waste and environmental services in North America. The Houston-based firm and its subsidiaries provide collection, transfer, recycling and resource recovery, and disposal services to nearly 20 million municipal, commercial, industrial, and residential customers in the United States, Canada, and Puerto Rico. The company's more than 43,000 employees helped it earn almost $12 billion in revenue in 2009. Waste Management runs a network of 390 collection operations, 345 transfer stations, 273 active landfill disposal sites, 17 waste-to-energy plants, 132 recycling plants, and 117 beneficial-use landfill gas projects. Combined with its wholly owned subsidiary, WM Recycle America, it is North America's leading recycler. The company's landfills provide more than 24,000 protected acres for wildlife.

HIS STORY

It's hard to be top dog and one of the guys. When you're a leader you can do all the outreach you want; you can regularly break bread with the rank and file, have an open-door policy, and insist that everyone call you by your first name. No matter how hard you try to be one of the guys, though, you'll always be the boss. There will always be things you don't hear from your employees, no matter how hard you try.

Larry O'Donnell prides himself on being part of the team. As president and chief operating officer, he'd tried hard to be accessible ever since he came to Waste Management in 2000. After a career in law, Larry joined the corporate ranks and within four years climbed to reach the COO role.

Despite or perhaps because of his not having started his career in the Waste Management trenches, Larry had gone out of his way to reach out to the company's frontline personnel. "I realized there were a lot of things I just didn't understand, and so I've made it my business to spend time in the field meeting with and talking to our people." Larry's aim in these conversations was to find out what made employees happy and unhappy on the job. "If I don't know about a problem, I can't do anything about it. We're all a team, and I want to be known as a team builder. We have different roles and responsibilities, but we either play hard together and succeed, or we fall short together and figure out what we need to do to win the next time."

Larry became known for carrying around a little pad on which he'd always make notes about the information and feedback he received from employees. "Every time I go to a location, I make it my business to sit with drivers and mechanics rather than managers at lunch. They've never held back, and I've always returned with a page full of notes."

Most of Larry's note taking, research, and spreadsheets serve to drive three major goals: boosting profitability, improving customer service, and maintaining safety. For all his genuine talk of team building, Larry obviously had a financial mandate, looking to make the company as much money as he can. "I'm always sending out performance targets and cost-cutting goals

PRODUCERS' NOTE
What You Didn't See

When Larry was growing up, his father owned a construction company and hardware store. Although the store has long since closed down, Larry's fond memories of his dad's business shone through when he took us to visit the site of the original location. Larry showed us around the building, now little more than a dilapidated warehouse, he had not visited in nearly 30 years.

Larry first started working for his dad's company at age 17 after a back injury derailed his promising football career. Rather than let him mope around the house, Larry Sr. took him into the fold of the family business. The very next year, Larry rose to the rank of foreman, overseeing the construction of three houses. It's no wonder that someone who exhibited such impressive leadership skills at just 18 years old would later find himself at the top of a major national corporation.

from my office. Increased efficiency translates into saving jobs." But efficiency alone isn't enough to stand out. "Previously we didn't feel like our service was any better than any of our competitors, so we've tried to focus on our customers more." But the goal that was closest to Larry's heart was safety. That's because it's personal.

"If I don't know about a problem, I can't do anything about it. We're all a team, and I want to be known as a team builder."

With pleasure in his voice, Larry says his son is the joy of his life, and his wife, Dare, is the source of his strength. His daughter, Linley, is clearly his inspiration. "She was born totally normal. During a routine test she threw up and aspirated, causing a lot of brain damage. It was really the result of a doctor not following proper procedure. We brought her home thinking we were bringing her home to die." Thankfully, Linley is still very much alive. The bubbly 25-year-old lives in a special home care facility at which Larry spends a great deal of time volunteering. It's easy to see they share a very special father-daughter connection. While his daughter's accident had a profound effect on him personally, it's also been a motivating force in his preoccupation with safety. "As a result of what happened to Linley, I never want to work at a company that I'm responsible for where people don't know how to follow the proper and safe procedures. We don't even begin our meetings without having a safety briefing."

It's more than just a question of the individual employee's safety: repercussions of unsafe procedures can reach far wider.

"If we drive our trucks unsafely and there's an accident, it's not just the people directly involved who are injured; families and communities are affected as well."

Larry was eager to go undercover to see how well his three goals had been absorbed into the culture of the company. But he also wanted the world to see the kind of people who work for his company. "I don't know if it's because of *The Sopranos,* but some of the public thinks everyone in our industry is connected to the mob and that our frontline folks are ex-cons," he explained. "We've got an unbelievable workforce, lots of whom take these very tough jobs so they can be home early for their families. I hoped going undercover would correct some of those mistaken notions."

This undercover adventure wasn't Larry's first time walking in his employees' boots: only one year prior, Larry took the test for his commercial driver's license so that he could drive his company's vehicles and get a sense for what some of his employees go through. On the day of his road test, however, he arrived early at one of the company's facilities to pick up a truck and found dozens of drivers already gathered around wishing him luck. Everyone seemed to know what he was doing. When he returned triumphant, the staff greeted him with a celebratory cake. Although the support of

"I never want to work at a company that I'm responsible for where people don't know how to follow the proper and safe procedures."

his employees was gratifying, Larry knew they were giving him special treatment. Despite all his well-intentioned efforts and candid conversations, Larry was still very much the boss in his employees' eyes. Going undercover would give him a chance to avoid that extra attention and see things he otherwise wouldn't.

JOB #1

Waste Not, Want Not

Recycling Line Sorter, Material Recovery Facility (MRF), Syracuse NY

Larry chose to start his undercover adventure at an MRF because recycling is such a significant part of the company's business, although in the economic downturn, margins were contracting. Wearing a watch cap to ward off the upstate New York chill, Larry arrived to do a typical assignment for an entry-level or temporary employee—working a sorting line.

Sandy, a line leader at the MRF, was to be Larry's boss for the day. Although she'd been at Waste Management for only three years, the 50-year-old Sandy brought to her job 20 years of prior experience running a line at a Nestlé USA factory. Despite Larry's already being dressed in his coveralls and wearing a hard hat and gloves, Sandy handed him additional safety gear for his assignment: ear plugs to minimize the noise and a pair of protective sleeves to avoid being stuck with needles or cut by glass. "When do we get paid?" asked Larry, very much in Randy character. "Thursdays," replied an unsuspecting Sandy.

As the mass of waste material rushed down the belt, Sandy patiently explained to Larry the color-coded bins into which cardboard, plastic, and trash must be separated from recyclables. She then stood behind him to check that he'd grasped what she'd told him. "Cardboard," said Sandy as he missed a big piece. Moment later, "Cardboard!" As the belt sped past, Sandy repeatedly called out to Larry, pointing out the cardboard and trash he missed . . . and missed. "Cardboard!!" Embarrassed, Larry attributed his failures to the speed of the belt. He grew more embarrassed when Sandy explained, "You're working on the slowest of the four belts."

Finally, Larry started demonstrating some proficiency, so Sandy moved him to one of the faster-moving belts. Sandy likes to think the best of people. She was being overoptimistic. Larry's heart raced as he tried to keep up at the new belt. "I was panicking, trying to keep an eye out for the cardboard and pull it off the belt so it didn't jam the machine. I was sweating bullets," he admitted, "because I know how expensive that equipment is." The alarm sounded. Larry's worst fears materialized. The belt ground to a halt. It was jammed with cardboard. Kindly, Sandy chose not to single Larry out. Instead, she sent the crew for their lunch break while the machine was cleared.

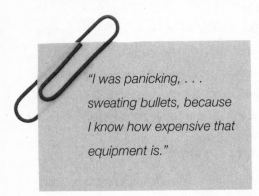

"I was panicking, . . . sweating bullets, because I know how expensive that equipment is."

Feeling awful about his mistake, Larry tried to confess that he was the machine-jamming culprit, when suddenly Sandy leaped up from their table and ran across the lunch room to the time clock as if her life depended on it. Everyone had to punch right back in at the 30-minute mark, or else they'd be docked two minutes for every minute they were late, Sandy explained to a puzzled Larry. Stunned, Larry tried to find out more about a policy he'd never heard of or approved. But before he could do anything, it was time to get back to the line. Larry spent the rest of the afternoon trying to ensure that he wasn't responsible for another jam.

"That kind of discovery was a great example of the benefits of being undercover. What Sandy described wasn't our time clock policy," Larry explained afterwards. The amount of pay that employees were meant to be docked for being late was much less. The policy hadn't been communicated properly. "I know Kevin, the manager of the facility. There was no way he would have implemented that kind of policy." It's also unlikely that Sandy or one of her crew would have ever brought up the issue if Larry had been there on an official visit. Larry's other revelation of the day was discovering how draining the noise and pace of the work was, combined with the mind-numbing repetitiveness and the pressure not to cause a jam. "I had no idea this job was going to be so physically demanding and mentally exhausting. My back was hurting like you couldn't believe. I wasn't sure I was going to be able to get to the next location." He did, but it wasn't Larry at his most alert who arrived at his next job.

JOB #2

A Bird in the Hand Is Worth Two in the Bush
Trash Collector, Central Landfill, Pompano Beach FL

Larry arrived at his next job at Waste Management's landfill facility in Pompano Beach, Florida, after only four hours of sleep. His boss was to make sure he'd stay awake. Walter is a 20-year veteran at Waste Management, having climbed from beautification and landscaping to fulfilling his childhood dream of becoming a heavy equipment driver, something he'd wanted to do since the fifth grade when he saw a bulldozer in action outside his classroom. Because of the respect his skill and expertise command, and his authoritative presence, 55-year-old Walter is a mentor for most of the staff at the facility.

Walter had a seemingly simple job for Larry to do. Walter wanted Larry, armed with a spiked pole and a plastic bag, to pick up litter on the side of a hill. With a sweeping zigzag motion of his arm, Walter showed Larry the pattern he wanted him to follow as he worked his way up the grass-covered, treeless incline. Thinking it would be easy, Larry still felt compelled to ask Walter for advice on technique. "What kind of technique do you want?" Walter answered, looking perplexed. "It's not a big deal. Just sticking and holding paper and picking it up. It isn't rocket science."

It might as well have been for Larry. Thanks to the wind, the litter had a mind of its own, teasing Larry, fleeing from him as soon as he got close enough to spear it. When he did manage to finally catch some litter, the breeze made it hard for Larry to manipulate the plastic bag. Larry thought that if he worked walking up and down the hill, he could use the wind to his advantage, but Walter insisted Larry take the prescribed zigzag course. When Walter checked on him after a while, Larry had to confess that he wasn't meeting his supervisor's performance goals. "The bag does have a hole in the top, doesn't it?" Walter asked, only half in jest. "Randy, you're not cutting the mustard," he said bluntly as they broke for lunch.

PRODUCERS' NOTE
What You Didn't See

It's not easy to become someone else. While working in the landfill, it's important to maintain lines of communication. But what's even more important is to remember who's doing the communicating. We lost count of the times Larry radioed in with "Larry for Walter"—completely forgetting that everyone on-site knew him as Randy!

Because they didn't allow our crew to accompany Larry out in the landfill, all we could do was nervously watch on the monitors as Walter responded, "I'm not Larry! There's no Larry here! My name is Walter!" Luckily Larry corrected himself before Walter caught on, narrowly avoiding blowing his cover.

Keen to get the no-nonsense Walter to warm up to him, Larry asked about what he did outside of work. Walter explained that much of his time was taken up with medical care. "I'm on dialysis, and that takes up three days and three nights," he said, casually adding, "I've lost the functions in my kidneys." When Larry expressed admiration for Walter's ability to remain so physically active, Walter was not one for self-pity. "I let my spirit tell my body what's gonna happen: what I'm gonna do and what I'm not gonna do. Because if I let the body tell me what I'm gonna do, I'm not gonna do very much. When I see a perfectly healthy person dragging around, and I can go out there and work circles around him, that really pisses me off, because I wish I was him."

Larry took the not-so-subtle hint. It inspired him to give his litter collection another go. But out on the hillside, inspiration

"I felt miserable out there in that wind, knowing I wasn't getting the job done. Walter's the only person who's ever fired me."

turned out not to be enough. Despite Larry's best efforts, the wind, plastic bag, and paper maintained their dominance. Because Larry was unable to fill two bags in 10 minutes, a disappointed Walter called his trainee over and gave him the bad news. He was fired.

Later that evening at his motel, Larry was dejected and deflated. "I felt miserable out there in that wind, knowing I wasn't getting the job done. Walter's the only person who's ever fired me."

JOB #3

Multi-Multitasking

Scale Operator, High Acres Landfill, Fairport NY

Hoping to get his mind off being fired, Larry turned to his next job with a clear purpose: "We try to run our landfills with a small staff. I wanted to see if our cost-cutting measures have taken effect." Unexpectedly, Larry also got to see some of the unintended consequences of those measures.

Briefed beforehand by Jeff, the facility manager, Larry was told that his boss for the day was the glue that held the place together. Talk about an understatement. "You wore boots, buddy," said 29-year-old dynamo Jaclyn as soon as she met Larry. "I hope you can keep up. I'm a sneakers girl myself because I'm always running around." She wasn't kidding. After leading Larry on a whirlwind tour of the tasks she has to accomplish in the course of the day in her roles as office manager and administrative assistant to the facility manager, Jaclyn led Larry to the scale building, where she also served as a scale operator and scale supervisor. She coached Larry through the process of weighing trucks when they arrived and then again when they departed to determine the proper charge. The line of trucks began to back up, but Jaclyn remained patient. When she did take over from Larry, she began fielding calls simultaneously. "The phone was ringing and she was entering stuff in the computer while chatting with the driver and telling me how to do things," Larry recalled in amazement. "She took multitasking to a whole new level."

Chatting on their way back to the office, Jaclyn said she felt proud that the company knew they could count on her. "I don't do it for the money, since I'm making the same salary as when I was just the administrative assistant. Life is what you make out of it." As they got to know each other over the course of the day, Jaclyn revealed that she had a total hysterectomy at age 21 and had battled and beaten five forms of cancer before she was 25. Not looking for sympathy, she quickly added, "Someday I'm gonna run this place." Learning he didn't have any family or friends nearby, Jaclyn invited Larry to come to her home for dinner that evening.

Over a dinner of spaghetti and meatballs, Larry discovered that Jaclyn, her husband, and their daughter share their home with Jaclyn's father, sister, and brother-in-law. After her busy day working at the landfill, Jaclyn came home to do the accounting, billing, and payroll for her husband's business. But the most troubling news was that the family's dream home was now up for sale because a recent reassessment had made the tax bills unaffordable on the family's income.

Larry was touched at Jaclyn's generosity toward him, a new employee without a friend in town. He was also troubled at the thought of her family's financial predicament. "I felt so bad for Jaclyn's family that I knew I had to get the ball rolling on solving her problem before I left for my next undercover location." Arranging to meet with Jeff, her manager, in secret in the parking lot before moving on to his next location, Larry learned that Jaclyn was having to do so many jobs because the landfill was shorthanded. Larry made it clear he'd taken a personal interest in Jaclyn's situation. He asked Jeff to put together some ideas for helping her move up in the organization.

JOB #4

The Battlefield of Poop

Port-O-Let Cleaner, Fairgrounds, Houston TX

"The job you're going to be doing is cleaning toilets." As Gilbert, Waste Management's site manager, spoke, Larry's face dropped. "These toilets don't flush. So when somebody goes in there, whatever they leave stays behind." This was a job Larry knew he needed to check out. It just wasn't one he was looking forward to experiencing.

Fred, Larry's boss for the day, was a 63-year-old with the energy of someone half his age. A bear of a man, whose imposing frame is softened by an omnipresent smile and infectious laugh, Fred had turned down chances to return to driving a residential garbage truck because he liked cleaning Port-O-Lets. He'd been doing it for 10 years.

As soon as they were driving down the road, heading for the first of several Port-O-Let locations at the giant fairgrounds, Fred let Larry in on his unique approach to the job. "We're like hunters. We see our prey. We creep up on 'em." Pulling up to a row of Port-O-Lets, Fred warned Larry, "We don't know what's in there. But we know it's trouble." As he opened the door of a stall to reveal a toilet soiled and covered with used wet tissue, Fred announced, "This is destiny." Even when having to clean a particularly foul-smelling stall, Fred kept his humor. "That is not from a human," he joked. "There's an animal in there."

Just as Fred and Larry were getting into a team rhythm, Gilbert arrived. "You've got about eight minutes to get out of here and get over to the VIP area." Fred told Larry to pick up the pace while he vacuumed the next stall. "Make it dance, Randy! Make it dance!" The hose bounced around as Larry hurried to empty the tank. On their way to the next site, Fred's banter continued. "This ain't just a job; it's an adventure. I call

 PRODUCERS' NOTE
What You Didn't See

It's easy to appreciate how Fred's great attitude made a dirty job palatable, even through the distance of a TV screen. But you had to actually be there to fully understand the scope of Fred's high spirits, given the intensely unsavory working conditions. While filming at the Houston Rodeo, three members of our crew lost their respective lunches from being around the smell.

it the Battlefield of Poop. Good soldiers endure. Even if you get a little splatter on you, you're wounded, but you keep going."

Looking back, Larry still couldn't get over what an impact an upbeat attitude and good humor could make: he'd actually enjoyed himself cleaning Port-O-Lets. "Fred takes a job most people consider nasty and he turned it into something fun. I don't think I've laughed so hard for that length of time doing any other job in my life."

JOB #5

Lifting Spirits as Well as Trash Cans

Garbage Truck Helper, Trash Hauling Company, Rochester NY

Larry chose to spend his last day undercover working a trash collection route in New York. It was the job he'd spent the most time studying and analyzing over the years, not the least because residential garbage truck drivers are the public faces of the company.

As dawn broke, Larry was introduced to Janice, his boss for the day. A short, spunky 49-year-old grandmother, Janice is a rarity at Waste Management as a female garbage truck driver. She's been with Waste Management for six years, having previously driven for a competitor. Janice began her working life as a geriatric nurse, but has come to love driving a garbage truck. With an enthusiastic "Let's get out there and pick up some trash," Janice took Larry on a route he was surprised to learn was made up of more than 300 houses.

Not long into the route, Janice received a call on her radio from a supervisor, checking up on her progress. "We're supposed to do our route the same way every day. I can be out here 12 or 13 hours, and they're calling me asking, 'What are you doing out there?' I'm working, for crying out loud. If some procedure comes up and we don't agree with it, we're told that's the way corporate wants it, so that's how it's going to be." Outwardly commiserating with her, Larry knew he was the one at corporate who has been driving productivity. "I felt terrible that I had created policies that were causing her not to enjoy her job."

It wasn't just corporate edicts that Janice revealed frustrated her and the other drivers. She explained that supervisors were often in the field, watching drivers work. She felt spied on. As one of the authors of the policy, Larry knew all about those field observations. "But I didn't know any of our drivers felt like they were being spied on. That's not what the policy was supposed to be about." Larry had previously heard firsthand from drivers who saw the observations as a good method to get a fresh perspective on ways to streamline their jobs.

Continuing along the route, Janice opened up to Larry about one of the other difficulties of her job. "It's a good company and everything, but I don't think it's female friendly." As they pulled up to their next stop and got out of the cab to load the trash, Janice showed Larry what she meant. Opening one of the side storage bins of the truck, she took out a coffee can with a plastic cover and handed it to Larry. "When you're a female working on one of these garbage trucks, this is your outhouse." Larry didn't understand at first, so Janice spelled it out for him: "I can't keep breaking off the route all the time to use the restroom. That would add too much time." Larry was shocked and embarrassed, not just by what Janice had to go through, but because he'd never thought about how the company's female drivers had to deal with being out on the road when nature called.

As Janice steered the truck onto yet another block, a smile came to her face, and all her frustrations seemed to disappear. She told Larry they were getting to a stretch of the route where he'd be able to meet some of her favorite customers: "These are the people who look forward to seeing me every week." It was obvious the feeling was mutual. At one house, an older woman was waiting by the curb to embrace Janice and give her a bottle of cream soda, her favorite. Further up the street, two other customers came out to say hello. Even the dogs looked happy to see Janice. Finally, at the end of the block, an exuberant middle-aged woman with short curly brown hair bounded out her door as Janice's truck approached. Again there was a warm embrace, and Janice introduced Larry to Karen, who's developmentally disabled. Karen sang Janice's praises, reading a letter she'd written about her favorite trash collector. Listening to Karen recite her letter about Janice, knowing how much trouble she'd gone through to write it and then read it to them, made Larry think of his own daughter. He was moved to tears.

Larry never expected to have an emotional moment on the back of a garbage truck, but neither did he think he'd lay awake at night questioning his approach to a job he thought he knew inside and out. "Our customers don't see me; they see Janice. She wanted to spend time with customers, but she also had to meet productivity targets. I'd created policies that could keep her from providing great customer service. There was something wrong with the way I'd been approaching productivity. I didn't realize the impact it could have on our drivers. All of that came right out of my office. It came right from me. I needed to fix it."

HE REVEALS THE TRUTH

Eager to address everything he'd seen and learned during his covert time in the field, Larry met with the company's leadership team on his first day back in Houston. He was pleased at how the message of safety had become part of the company's culture. "At every job, my coworkers were constantly reminding me, as the new guy, what I needed to do to keep from getting hurt." He was also glad to know how many of the company's initiatives toward boosting profitability were working out. But he was concerned about the issues that he knew needed correcting. Employees shouldn't feel spied on. Waste collection routes needed rest breaks. Staff shouldn't be asked to do too many jobs. "Productivity is important," he affirmed, "but we need to find a way to balance that with not frustrating good employees who are trying to provide the high level of customer service we're looking for."

He then revealed his true identity to each of his "bosses" from the previous week . . .

When Fred learned that his assistant on the Battlefield of Poop was the company president, he broke out in an uproarious laugh. With both men grinning ear to ear, Larry told Fred how great it was working with him: "The positive approach and attitude you bring to your job makes such a big difference. All I could think was, *How can we tap into the feeling you have, and help others in our company share that kind of excitement?* I'd like you to come up and speak to our senior leadership team and help us brainstorm." Fred was too touched to be able to make a joke. "I'm so honored. It would be a privilege, a real privilege to do that, Larry. I promise you I'll put everything I have into it."

Janice, upon learning that the helper with whom she'd shared her frustrations was actually the boss, was worried. After all, she hadn't pulled many punches when candidly expressing her views on management's oversight practices. Larry reassured her and described what she taught him. "Janice, there was one thing you said that just hit me right between the eyes. You kept talking about 'Houston' and 'corporate.' You know who you were talking about? *Me.* I got to experience firsthand the frustrations that some of the decisions I've made are causing you and other drivers." He explained that some field managers were being retrained to use and present their observations as positive coaching sessions, rather than searches for flaws. Larry then addressed the specific difficulties Janice faced as a female driver. "You have my commitment that I'll get those fixed. We're going to form a task force to work on ways we can make this an environment that works for you." Janice appreciated Larry's recognition of the hurdles she faced in doing her job. "He made a commitment and that's awesome. I'm going to hold him to it."

Next Larry met with Walter, who looked momentarily disconcerted but quickly recovered, joking that Randy, "cleaned up real good." Larry confided that Walter's personal story touched him deeply. "You've been on dialysis for almost 20 years, and yet you have such a positive attitude. I'd like to create a program that will give you paid time off, so you can help other folks going through medical treatment. You're a very inspirational guy." Walter, uncomfortable at receiving such praise, could only respond by returning it. "It means a lot to me that you came down to work with us. Most bosses in high positions don't even take the time to say hello."

Sandy looked stunned when she realized that the rookie recycling sorter who jammed one of the machines was actually the president of the company. Larry homed in on what, for him, was the vital lesson he came away with. "Do you remember when you and I were having lunch? You got up and bolted out of the lunch room because you thought you had to clock back in exactly on the 30-minute mark. Well, I knew that wasn't our policy, and that really bothered me. So I'm going to talk to Kevin, the facility manager, and we're going to get that fixed."

And true to his word, Larry called Kevin into his office and explained the anxiety Sandy and some other employees were experiencing over the time clock. The misunderstanding about how the docking policy should work for employees who were late was straightened out, and Larry felt gratified that he'd been able to uncover and deal with an employee frustration.

Jaclyn, the overburdened office manager, was speechless when it dawned on her that she had had the COO over for spaghetti and meatballs. "Your personal story really hit me," Larry admitted. "You're doing several people's jobs at once, yet you don't complain. You just get it done." Larry had good news for her. She would become a salaried employee, get a pay increase, and become eligible for bonuses. She would also become a supervisor, whose first job was to a hire her own replacement, so that she could take on more responsibility. "I can't describe how good it feels for all my hard work to have been noticed and rewarded," Jaclyn said as she fought to hold back tears.

Finally, Larry shared his undercover experiences with all of the headquarters and local staff. Video highlights showed some of the moving moments with each employee, as well as his own humbling shortcomings—being unable to keep up with the sorting line and failing as a litter picker. Still relishing the moment, Larry was also able to laugh at himself before he turned serious with the assembled group: "In my role as COO, there are many policies I create that you all have to live with. Now that I've actually made a connection with the people who do the hard jobs at this company, I'm going to be a better manager. I have a whole new appreciation of the impact my decisions have on you folks."

"If you ask employees, not just in our company but in every company, what they want more of, money doesn't top the list. At the top of the list is always recognition."

Larry also learned that there is a level of insight into the problems of employees that an executive will never achieve unless he's able to relate to his team members as a peer rather than a boss. For all of Janice's spunkiness, it's unlikely she'd have shown Larry the coffee can she had to use as a urinal if she had known he was the president of the company.

Because it's not always possible to go undercover, Larry is more convinced than ever that it's vital to solicit input from employees and put the insights acquired into practice. "The people doing frontline jobs at a company know quite a bit about how to make things better. If you listen to them, and try to implement some of what they suggest, they will be so happy and engaged that it will make them feel even more a part of your team. People want to feel like they have a voice, that they have skin in the game. If they see they have a way to give insight into how to improve or fix something, you'll end up with a very high performing company.

"If you ask employees, not just in our company but in every company, what they want more of, money doesn't top the list. At the top of the list is always recognition. When you can do that in a way that's heartfelt and genuine, it can be very powerful. I really feel good about what we accomplished."

SINCE THE SHOW

★ People still come up to **Fred** and tell him how much they appreciate his attitude toward work. He left Waste Management to work in a hospital.

★ **Janice** held Larry to his promise and worked with his task force to create a more female-friendly work environment. She still has a long day, starting at 2:30 A.M., but is thrilled with the positive changes Larry put in place.

★ **Walter** became a health mentor to the entire company, and led several seminars, mentoring other employees about how to handle full-time work while also being on dialysis. Sadly, in August 2010, his health deteriorated, and he passed away.

★ After Larry helped **Sandy** and her crew straighten out the time clock policy, morale and production increased to the point where the plant won an award for excellence in recycling.

★ **Jaclyn** hired two people to replace her at the landfill and became a customer account manager. She and her family have been able to keep their home. Currently recovering from surgery related to her cancer, she's anxious to return to work.

★ In June 2010, **Larry** decided to leave Waste Management. He felt that he had achieved a great deal during his years with the company, but now had a desire to take on new challenges, this time as the chief executive of a company.

Larry felt that his *Undercover Boss* experience gave him the opportunity to learn many valuable business lessons. It also gave him an even greater sense of personal gratitude. "My family has had issues we've had to deal with, but there are lots of people who are really hurting, and have other issues that, fortunately, I haven't had to deal with. It was really a wake-up call about how blessed I've been in life."

WINGS, WOMEN, AND BEER

"My father could never adjust to modern ways of management. His generation managed by negative reinforcement, through fear. He taught me by my learning not to make his mistakes."

Coby Brooks
CEO, Hooters

Scotty Archer
Job Seeker

How We Found the Boss

The renowned Hooters restaurant chain is a brand defined by wings, beer, and scantily clad waitresses. While CEO Coby Brooks aims to promote a fun-loving environment for his customers, he is also committed to promoting a positive and rewarding work environment for his world-famous "Hooters Girls." As so many of his frontline staff are female, the undercover experience was always going to be a challenge for Coby, but he rolled up his sleeves and donned the white-and-orange Hooters T-shirt, even if it was a tight fit. Unbeknownst to many, Hooters is a family business that Coby's father, Robert, grew from a small base. Coby believed that going undercover would give him a chance to reflect on his father's legacy.

THE BOSS

Coby Brooks, president and CEO of Hooters of America, Inc., and Naturally Fresh, Inc.

HIS COVER

Scotty Archer, who is being filmed for a program that follows someone investigating potential career paths, because his family construction business is suffering in the recession.

HIS COMPANY

On April Fools' Day in 1983, six businessmen from Clearwater, Florida, opened a restaurant on a lark. The idea was simple: good food, cold beer, and beautiful women. A place where men could have a "good time" and not be thrown out. With attractive waitresses dressed in tight white tank tops and orange shorts (which would go on to become what the restaurant would be most identified with), they called their business Hooters and, in a far from subtle way, adopted an owl as its logo. Less than a year later, the original owners sold expansion and franchise rights to their concept to Atlanta businessman Robert Brooks, owner of Naturally Fresh, a manufacturer of condiments and salad dressings. Brooks, who got his start supplying packaged nondairy creamer and salad dressings to airlines, took the politically incorrect Hooters concept and turned it into a global business. Today, Hooters of America has locations in 44 states and 27 countries. With the opening of a restaurant on Guam, the company has taken to pointing out that, like the British Empire, the sun never sets on Hooters.

The original concept, and even the original uniform of the Hooters Girl, has changed little over the years. Female sex appeal, in a retro 1980s package, remains essential to the Hooters business model, and the company argues that Hooters Girls are no less socially acceptable than Dallas Cowboy cheerleaders, *Sports Illustrated* swimsuit models, or Radio City's Rockettes. Hooters bills its outlets as "neighborhood" rather than "family" restaurants. Males between the ages of 25 and 54 make up almost 70 percent of Hooters customers. It welcomes women and children, but does not specifically market to them. In an attempt to counter the perception that it's exploitative, Hooters of America cites its proactive efforts in addressing issues of sexual harassment and its extensive community outreach and philanthropic work. Since 1992, its Hooters Community Endowment Fund has raised more than $8 million for a variety of charities. In 2006, the company established a $2 million breast cancer research grant in honor of one its employees. In 2009, after the death of the husband of a Hooters Girl, it established a fund to honor Special Forces service members and military families.

HIS STORY

Most people's lives are unplanned. Fate and circumstances conspire to push people in directions they didn't anticipate or desire.

Coby Brooks never expected to be CEO of Hooters. The 40-year-old, divorced father of three worked in one or another of his father's businesses from his first summer job all the way through high school. But Coby didn't see the family business as his calling and planned to pursue a career in law enforcement. Coby and his father, Bob, had diametrically opposed styles. Bob was hard driving, gruff, and aggressive, whereas Coby is calm, soft spoken, and thoughtful. Coby's older brother, Mark, was the obvious heir apparent. After graduating college, Coby was about to interview for law enforcement jobs when his father pleaded with him to come work for Hooters for one year before pursuing other interests. "My father had me in the car with him and kept driving around trying convince me. I knew that the only way I'd ever get out of the car was to agree." In 1992, Coby signed on to work at headquarters for one year. It was a fateful year. Coby's brother, Mark, died in a private plane crash, along with champion NASCAR driver Alan Kulwicki, whose car was sponsored by Hooters. Driven to help the family through the crisis, Coby resolved to stay in the business.

Around the same time, the company was involved in a series of high-profile lawsuits, including one claiming discrimination because Hooters wouldn't hire male waiters. The six founders and Bob had frequent fights over the terms of the licensing and franchising agreement. And Bob divorced Coby's mother after more than 30 years of marriage. "My father and I had a lot of fundamental differences of opinion, a lot of arguments and disagreements. From day one to the day he passed away," said Coby tactfully, "our relationship was very contentious." By 1999, the strain of working for the competitive and combative Bob brought Coby to the breaking point. He left for what amounted to a two-year cooling-off period. Relations improved enough for him to return full-time to the company, but even this rapprochement didn't prepare Coby for what happened next. In 2003, Bob called all the managers to a meeting at the headquarters in Atlanta and announced that the current president of the company was leaving. Coby would be taking over his job. It was as much a surprise to Coby as it was to everyone else.

Except for a high-profile disagreement over his father's decision to go into the airline business, the generational transition went surprisingly smoothly. Coby has worked on evolving rather than changing the business. He's made some upgrades to the menu and added mixed drinks to the restaurant's original offerings of just beer and wine. Coby has worked to modernize the facilities, putting in more comfortable seating and newer video screens, and providing wifi. Much of Coby's personal efforts have gone toward improving relations with the company's franchise owners, who sometimes felt at odds with Bob's approach. "My father could never adjust to modern ways of management," Coby admitted. "His generation managed by negative reinforcement, through fear. He taught me by my learning not to make his mistakes." Coby said the shift in management style has been well received and effective, as the company has now expanded to become a $1 billion business with more than 450 locations, 120 of which are company owned.

Bob passed away in 2006, and Coby remains determined both to stay at the helm of the business his father built and to keep the company privately owned. As if that weren't enough, he's also facing the same kind of problems as every other business: "We're in a terrible economy and sales are down," he conceded.

Coby's serene personality and sober style have apparently enabled him to set aside all the outside turmoil and focus on the day-to-day demands of his business. He decided to go under-cover to get a close-up, unbiased view of frontline operations to see what the company can do to make sure it's better positioned to weather the recession. "When you come from upper levels of the company and visit restaurants, it's very difficult to get honest feedback and reactions. You're never sure you're getting the truth or the whole story. Now's the time I need to be able to uncover things I normally wouldn't get access to."

Coby would uncover more than he probably wished.

JOB #1

Boot Camp Failure

Kitchen Staff, Hooters Restaurant, Dallas TX

With his picture a visible presence in all the chain's company-owned restaurants, Coby decided to work undercover in fran-chised stores only. He shaved his goatee and donned glasses, and lucked out when many of the upper-level franchise managers who might recognize him went on a retreat. His first job was at the chain's largest location, the 15,000-square-foot restaurant on the western side of downtown Dallas.

"It's obvious we put a lot of emphasis on the Hooters Girls, so I'm afraid we sometimes don't spend enough time looking into the back of the house. That's where the kitchen staff does all the hard work that makes Hooters Girls look so good." Although the company had initiated awards and recognition programs for kitchen crews, Coby was afraid that not all the franchisees had followed suit. Coby was also worried about being physically able to do the job. "The last time I worked in

a kitchen, other than the one in my house, was more than 20 years ago."

He was right to be concerned. The general manager, Dave, a former Marine and police officer, frankly told Coby he'd be "cannon fodder." His job would be to absorb the added work created by the dinner rush. Dave was quick with a friendly tease, but didn't let that get in the way of running the huge restaurant with military discipline. Constantly prodding and cajoling Coby to pick up the pace, Dave shifted the trainee from food prep to cleanup and back again as the need warranted. At various points during the shift, he warned that Coby's slow pace was creating traffic jams in the restaurant.

"Scotty was thrown into the meat grinder like everyone else who starts here," Dave admitted. "He wasn't fast enough." Dave took Coby aside, thanked him, and told him he should just go home. Coby had been more of a hindrance than a help. Other staff would have to be pulled out of the kitchen to finish up all the work Coby couldn't get to. "Why don't you keep the hat and the shirt as a reminder of why you don't want to lose the job you have now," Dave joked.

A physically exhausted Coby didn't seem too upset at the news that he probably wouldn't be invited back to the kitchen anytime soon. He appreciated that to keep a restaurant of that size from spiraling out of control, the manager had to run a tight ship with no room for anyone who couldn't keep up. Coby had anticipated how hard the job would be, but he did discover one thing that had changed since his own kitchen experience decades before. "I was surprised at how much the back of the house is a Latino culture today. I don't speak Spanish, so it was almost impossible for me to communicate with most of my coworkers.

Dave speaks enough Spanish to get by, but I think maybe we should provide our Anglo managers and assistant managers with training in rudimentary Spanish—even if it's just kitchen terminology and lingo—so they can communicate more effectively."

PRODUCERS' NOTE
What You Didn't See

Just as we were starting to shoot the Hooters episode, Coby's lower back started giving him problems. Although he didn't have a clue which jobs he would be performing for the company, Coby had an inkling that some of them would be pretty labor intensive, so he found a chiropractor who would do house calls to give him adjustments and allow him to continue his mission despite pain and strain.

The first night Coby checked into his rather sketchy (his words) hotel, this chiropractor showed up nervously not knowing what to expect. Let's just say the hotel looked more Bates Motel than Four Seasons. While waiting in his car, the chiropractor said that the nature of the hotel brought thoughts of a weird sort of police sting operation to his mind. But once he and Coby found one another, his concerns were washed away, and adjustments inside the hotel room–turned–chiropractic office became a nightly ritual.

Coby wasn't the only one working hard during the shoot—it was also a challenging shoot and long schedule for the crew. With a new understanding of the hardships that arise from working on set day after day, Coby introduced a few hardworking crew members to his chiropractor. At the end of the week, he arranged for them to get adjusted by the chiropractor in the hotel room as well!

JOB #2

Home Truths

Promotional Rep, Hooters Restaurant, Dallas TX

For his second undercover job, Coby returned to the same Dallas store. Luckily for Dave and the kitchen staff, Coby would this day be assigned to do promotional work out in the community with two Hooters Promo Girls, Amanda and Brittney.

Brittney gave Coby a bright orange Hooters warm-up to wear, and Amanda offered him his choice of T-shirts. "We have sizes extra-extra small, extra-small, and small. Which would you like?" When Coby explained that he didn't think he could fit into any of them, Amanda explained that since all female employees had to fit into them, so did he. After managing to squeeze into the small T-shirt, Coby and the two women set up post at a busy intersection. Offering sample boneless chicken wings and handing out flyers touting the restaurant's menu and specials, Amanda, Brittney, and Coby engaged passersby.

On the street in their full Hooters garb, it wasn't too long before they found themselves heckled. A few middle-aged guys announced they were looking for "beer, naked girls, and TV." Someone jested that he could understand that Amanda and Brittney were Hooters servers, but wondered what Coby did. Coby and the girls took it in stride, offered their own quips (when asked if he was a Hooters Girl, Coby countered that he "had the wrong parts").

Not all the interaction was so lighthearted. Brittney and Amanda found themselves questioned by other women as to whether they felt exploited. One couple admitted they'd been to a Hooters but didn't like it: the woman thought the chain exploited women, and the man said they couldn't justify taking their kids there. Another couple stopped by with similar comments: the man said he loved Hooters, but his female companion thought it was degrading to women.

Brittney and Amanda weren't strangers to this type of public reaction. Brittney told Coby that it was mostly due to the uniform. "When I first started and they handed me the uniform, I was like, 'Oh that's a joke. You want me to fit in it?' But it really isn't as bad as you think it's going to be."

One of the women on the street agreed that it was the scanty uniform that was her biggest problem with Hooters. Amanda defended the outfit, saying she felt fully clothed and that when she went swimming in public, she wore far more revealing garb. But the woman wasn't swayed. She wouldn't want her daughter or her sister to work in that kind of outfit.

Amanda and Brittney weren't embarrassed or deterred by the comments. As they walked back to the restaurant, Brittney remarked that whatever the woman thought, her husband would still come in. But Coby was troubled. He knew that Hooters was perceived as being sexist, but he had never before seen his employees having to confront this perception. "Seeing this back-and-forth firsthand was really eye opening. This is definitely a burden that lies on my shoulders. I've got to figure out some other way to bring more customers in without messing with the Hooters Girl uniform. We know we're not going to be accepted by 100 percent of the population. But if we can change just a few percent of people's minds it would make a huge difference. There's a lot of negative and bad things out there in the world, and honestly, Hooters isn't one of them."

> "Seeing this back-and-forth firsthand was really eye opening. This is definitely a burden that lies on my shoulders. . . . We know we're not going to be accepted by 100 percent of the population. But if we can change just a few percent of people's minds it would make a huge difference."

JOB #3

Table Manners

Assistant Manager, Hooters Restaurant, Arlington, TX

Having struggled working in the kitchen and as a Hooters Girl, Coby next tackled a job he felt confident he could perform: assistant manager. "The general manager of a store is like the coach of a team; he has to make sure everyone works together to reach their goal." Unfortunately, Coby found himself part of team in need of a different coach.

Beefy and cocky, Jimbo, a Hooters general manager for seven years, confidently proclaimed he'd take Coby under his wing and show him the ropes. Stressing that Hooters was all about the Hooters Girls, Jimbo had the girls line up for inspection before their shift. In a moment that seemed uncomfortable for everyone (except Jimbo), he went down the line, assessing each Hooters Girl's hair, makeup, nails, and uniform.

Typically some of the Hooters Girls prefer to be sent home after the lunch rush, because the thinner crowds of the

PRODUCERS' NOTE
What You Didn't See

We usually encourage our undercover bosses to transform themselves so as not to be recognized by their employees. But in North Arlington, Texas, Coby underwent one of the most adventurous transformations of the show—he became a Hooters Girl. A young waitress named Amanda (not to be confused with Amanda the promo girl who worked in the Dallas store) taught Coby everything he needed to know to be a successful server at Hooters.

However, there are some things about being a Hooters Girl one simply cannot teach. Coby certainly didn't get any free passes for being a male waiter—during his shift, he received a request to expose his "hooters" (Coby's standard response: "I was born without them!") and was complimented on his shapely rear end.

late afternoon mean fewer tips. Rather than choosing who got to leave early, Jimbo announced that they would have to play one of his "reindeer games." He made the girls compete in a food-eating contest, having them eat baked beans off plates while holding their hands behind their backs. The first one to clean her plate would earn the right to go home early. Although part of the Hooters system is to have the women engage in playful contests

"That was just inappro-priate and unacceptable behavior for anyone working for my company."

as entertainment for the patrons, Coby looked very uncomfortable. He questioned Jimbo's choice of game. "Hey, no rules," Jimbo responded. "The girls are spoiled; they're all prima donnas." With that as his explanation, Jimbo insisted on starting the contest, and all the waitresses had to play. "Hey, this isn't right," several of them objected. It was the most shocking behavior that any of our undercover bosses witnessed in the show's first season.

Stealing an opportunity to step outside the restaurant, an angry Coby phoned the owner of the franchise and left a message: "You've got a manager who's approaching and interacting with the girls in an unacceptable manner. I think it's a serious matter that needs some immediate action."

The normally imperturbable Coby struggled to hold his tongue and stay undercover. "If I could have broken cover, I would have grabbed Jimbo by the ear, pulled him aside, and had a very long, serious talk about how inappropriate his actions were. . . . That was just inappropriate and unacceptable behavior for anyone working for my company."

PRODUCERS' NOTE
What You Didn't See

Jimbo's management style put Coby in a difficult position. Coby felt strongly about protecting the Hooters Girls at this Texas location, but as CEO he also had to handle this through proper process. As the restaurant was a franchise operation, Coby didn't have the direct authority to hire or fire Jimbo.

JOB #4

A Gentler Way

Assistant Manager, Hooters Restaurant, Fort Worth TX

Having worked with two male managers with very opposite approaches, Coby's next undercover job gave him the chance to learn about the challenges facing female managers.

Following Marcee, the assistant general manager of the Fort Worth restaurant, on her rounds, Coby observed yet another management style: one no less effective than Dave's and far less confrontational than Jimbo's. Marcee patrolled the restaurant relentlessly, interceding when needed, whether the issue was as mundane as mopping up a spill or as potentially problematic as cutting off a noticeably intoxicated patron. Marcee's upbeat personality appealed to guests, and her supportive approach to employees, particularly the Hooters Girls, added a family tone to the staff dynamics.

Chatting with Marcee, Coby learned she was a mother of two girls, four and five, and had started her career working as a Hooters Girl herself. Marcee explained that being a woman, as well as having gone through what the women go through on the job, made it easy for her to connect with her staff. But even though that made for a more supportive, nurturing environment in the restaurant, the long, irregular hours of the work made for a stressful home life. "It's a constant juggle with my kids," she admitted. "I just try to spend as much time with them as I can."

Coby realized that there are some distinct advantages to having female managers. "Every year more and more women are becoming managers at our restaurants, and we're finding that the Hooters Girls often relate better to a female manager than a male manager. Women can run just as tight a ship as men, but they also can be better at explaining the Hooters concept than a man who doesn't wear makeup or spend as much time on his hair and appearance." However, because women are more often primary family caregivers, that also means female managers may be under more stresses and have more personal issues to deal with than their male counterparts.

JOB #5

Reconnecting with the Past
Line Worker, Naturally Fresh Factory, Atlanta GA

Coby finished his undercover mission, not at another Hooters, but at the Naturally Fresh factory, which makes the sauces, salad dressings, and dips for Hooters restaurants. Bob Brooks loved

Naturally Fresh, often calling it his baby. He was famous for walking the halls and factory floor, chatting with employees, many of whom he'd known for years. Coby was concerned that morale might have suffered since the death of his father, who was a constant presence.

Coby practically grew up at the factory because both his parents worked there. However, he hadn't been back since he was 17. The management team that operates Naturally Fresh is separate from the Hooters management team, and Coby doesn't have a day-to-day role in the organization. Still, Coby knew this would be the most difficult job for him in terms of staying undercover, because so many people still at the plant had known him since he was young. What he didn't anticipate was that it would also be the most difficult job emotionally.

To pull off this undercover mission, Coby enlisted the help of Patti, the plant's business manager, and Chip, the sales director. They snuck Coby in through the loading dock and gave him a hairnet to cover his head and a set of safety lenses over his eyeglasses. Chip then hustled the fully covered Coby through the factory floor to work alongside Ricky, a newer employee, filling large, commercial-size containers of Hooters Medium Hot Wing Sauce.

As the two men worked the equipment, Coby quizzed Ricky about the company, and learned that employees at the factory remembered Bob fondly and missed his presence. "He died right after I started," Ricky explained, "but I heard he was a really nice guy." Taking a break together, Coby learned that employees felt the company had gone downhill since his father's death. "People say it used to be a pleasure to work here, but now a lot of them don't want to be here." Coby couldn't resist asking what people thought about the new owner, the old boss's son. "They're probably hating the guy right now," Ricky guessed. "But I don't know if they know him."

Coby felt as though he'd been punched in the stomach. "I felt bad when Ricky said yeah, the son's taking over, and everything's falling apart. . . . It hurt. I felt like I've let down the Brooks family name." Sneaking through the executive offices, Coby sat down with Patti in his father's old office to talk about what he'd learned. The setting didn't make him feel any better. "It was eerie walking in there. It felt like my dad was going to appear and say something at any minute. No one can fill his office." Patti confirmed much of what Coby had learned from Ricky. She was pleased to hear of his plan to be more of a physical presence at the plant in the future. "Seeing a family presence would mean a lot to the long-timers and the newcomers as well." Coby conceded he didn't expect to fill his father's shoes. "That would be impossible. All I want to do is make him proud," he said with a cracking voice.

"It was eerie walking in there. It felt like my dad was going to appear and say something at any minute. No one can fill his office. . . . All I want to do is make him proud."

HE REVEALS THE TRUTH

On his return to headquarters, Coby endured some good-natured ribbing from his executive team over losing his beard. "I would have shaved my whole head for the experience I went through," he offered, undeterred. After discussing all the positive moments, Coby turned to the subject of Jimbo. "I found a manager who's not respectful of the girls. He somehow slipped through the cracks, and he has the potential to do a lot of damage." The team wondered whether retraining could salvage Jimbo's career with Hooters. Moving to the poor morale at Naturally Fresh, Coby explained that although he couldn't bring his father back, he would do more to reassure them that ownership still cared. Choking up, he told his executive team, "After this week, I love doing my job a hell of a lot more than I did seven days ago."

With his briefing over, Coby turned to revealing his true identity to those with whom he'd worked during his undercover week.

Amanda and Brittney, though initially stunned to learn that their promotional assistant actually owned the company, quickly recovered their poise. When Coby jokingly thanked them for the tight shirt, Amanda said that now he knows what they go through every day. Recalling the mixed reception they received during their promotional effort, Coby asked the two women to help his marketing department develop a campaign to educate the public about Hooters' community and charitable efforts. Both were thrilled. "It would be awesome to get people to see we're not just Hooter Girls," Brittney explained. "We're not just girls who serve wings and beer—we're real people," added Amanda.

Dave, smiling and showing a less intense side of his personality than was on display at work, was thrilled to have the CEO tell him what a great job he was doing. Coby added that he'd be making a $50,000 donation to Operation Homefront in Dave's name. "I was very happy with that. He's going to be making a big donation in my name to a cause that's near and dear to my heart, helping out the people in the military and their families."

Marcee was touched as Coby described how concerned he was with the level of stress in her life. "Restaurants are inherently stressful, and I could tell how tired you were. We need to make sure we don't lose the good people, like you, in our system. One thing I can do for you now is send you and your family on a long vacation, anywhere in the world, all expenses paid." As a tearful Marcee thanked him, Coby said all she had to do was tell him where she wanted to go, send him some pictures, and come back rejuvenated. "For him to actually give me the opportunity to spend more time with my kids is just awesome. It's more than I would ever have expected anyone to do for me."

After revealing his true identity to Jimbo, Coby got right to the point. "The way that you interact with the girls is inappropriate. . . . You're not giving them the respect they need." Telling Jimbo that he'd crossed the line, Coby said the manager needed to apologize to his staff. Jimbo tried to defend himself. "If I'm too competitive and if I'm too harsh, man, it works. Shame on me if it's a bad thing being über-competitive. I do have a track record of building sales and—" Coby cut Jimbo off, saying he could talk about profits all he wanted, but the bottom line that mattered was being respectful. "I'm a proud father of three children, two of which are girls. I've always said I'd have no problem with my girls working in Hooters. But to be honest with you, I would have a tough time letting my girls work under your management." That seemed to strike a chord in Jimbo, who claimed he understood what Coby was saying and would take it to heart.

With his private reveals, pleasant and unpleasant, behind him, Coby next had to tell the rest of the company about his undercover experiences. In an outdoor celebration, reminiscent of the many opening celebrations that he emcees all over the world, Coby told the story of his undercover week. However, this time his speech was more revelatory of a new vision than celebratory of an old one. "We're a great company, but we're going to make it even better. We're going to work on time management to help out single moms and single dads. We're going to start a new marketing campaign to show the world who Hooters Girls really are. We're going to talk about the Hooters Girls who are now doctors, lawyers, movie stars; the women who've worked for us and gone on to do amazing things. We're going to show that they are people, not just Hooters Girls. From the bottom of my heart, and for my father, thank you all for being part of the Hooters family."

"Now that my journey has concluded, I know why I do my job. I don't think I ever did before. I'm working for my dad's legacy."

In the afterglow of the event, surrounded by pomp and glitz he hadn't pursued, the man who never planned to be head of such a prominent company had a moment of private providence. "Now that my journey has concluded, I know why I do my job. I don't think I ever did before. I'm working for my dad's legacy. My dad was never a man of complimentary words. But on rare occasions he would look at you and give you a little nod or a little wink. I think I probably would have earned a wink today."

SINCE THE SHOW

✯ **Dave** is still running the west-end Dallas Hooters with military precision. This past summer, he presented Operation Homefront with a $50,000 check in his honor, part of the company's ongoing efforts to support that charity.

✯ **Amanda** and **Brittney** are both playing an active part in what has come to be called Operation Orange Pride. Designed to publicly promote the achievements and good works of Hooters Girls, past and present, it is also developing into an esteem-building effort for Hooter Girls across the globe.

✯ **Jimbo** formally apologized to his staff. He subsequently left the company.

✯ **Marcee** and her daughters were treated to a weeklong, first-class stay in Marco Island, FL. Upon her return, she was offered and accepted another job within the company that lets her spend more time with her children.

✯ **Coby** remains president and CEO of Hooters of America. True to his word, he has been visiting the Naturally Fresh factory as often as his schedule permits, to walk the floor and halls and speak with employees there. Morale has improved.

His undercover experience has left him more committed than ever to break down the communication barriers that exist between executives and frontline employees throughout his organization. "We've implemented a program which requires all of our executives to twice a year rotate out into the field and participate at levels they aren't accustomed to, in order to get a sense for the real-world problems and issues facing our employees."

Despite having had to confront with Jimbo what many consider the worst situation faced by any of the Undercover Bosses, Coby's a believer in the exercise. "If you go undercover in your organization, you can't be scared about what you may find. You have to accept that whatever you find, it's better that you've found it. It's just like dealing with what life gives you. What matters is *how* you deal with it on a professional and personal level."

> "I truly believe that if you take care of your people, and treat them well, your bottom line will work out."

It's on that personal level that Coby took away yet another lesson, one that has helped him put his own recent turbulence in perspective. "Everyone has problems. Every family is dysfunctional in some way. Going undercover helped me see that my problems aren't anywhere near as severe as those many people face. It was quite humbling. Since going undercover I find that I'm not dwelling as much on my own issues, and I'm trying to focus on others. I truly believe that if you take care of your people, and treat them well, your bottom line will work out."

THE NECESSITIES OF LIFE

"Being able to offer thousands of people a pathway to their American Dream is part of our corporate DNA."

Joe DePinto
CEO, 7-Eleven

Danni Rossi
Job Seeker

How We Found the Boss

Most of us have visited a 7-Eleven convenience store at some point in our lives—it is, after all, the world's largest convenience chain. But most of us casual shoppers never really think about the volume of work and logistics required to deliver the convenience we rely on. It was no surprise that we found a proud military veteran at the helm of the massive 7-Eleven enterprise. CEO Joe DePinto is devoted to supporting his company's franchised locations. He leaped at the opportunity to go undercover and get an insider's view of what his franchisees and customers experience every day.

THE BOSS

Joe DePinto, president and CEO of 7-Eleven, Inc.

HIS COVER

Danny Rossi, who lost his real estate job and is looking for new opportunities, and who's being followed by film crew shooting a TV show on entry-level jobs.

HIS COMPANY

7-Eleven stores aren't everywhere, but they're getting close. The Dallas-based company has edged out McDonald's as the largest franchise in the world, with more than 38,500 outlets in 16 countries. The now ubiquitous convenience store got its start in Dallas in 1927 when an ice company employee named Joe Thompson also started selling milk, eggs, and bread. The enterprising Thompson eventually bought the Southland Ice Company and opened stores throughout the city. Thompson's stores were open from 7 A.M. to 11 P.M., which was extraordinary for that time. By 1946, those hours had turned into the chain's name: 7-Eleven. In the early 1960s, the chain began keeping some stores open 24 hours. Today, most 7-Eleven locations are open 24 hours a day, seven days a week, 365 days a year. Japanese firm Seven-Eleven Japan and its parent company Ito-Yokado first helped stave off a 7-Eleven bankruptcy in the late 1980s, then gained a controlling interest in the early 1990s, and finally took the company private, making it a subsidiary of a holding company called Seven & i Holdings. The company employs a variety of operating models around the world. In the United States and Canada, its stores are franchised or corporately owned. In Mexico, its outlets are part of a joint venture. And in the rest of the world, the company typically enters markets using licensees or master franchisees. As it is privately held, profit information is not public. However, the London-based research firm Planet Retail estimates that the company had 2009 revenues of about $17 billion.

Despite its global presence and international pedigree, 7-Eleven remains an American cultural fixture. Its signature Slurpee and Big Gulp products have gained cult followings. The company has even embraced being parodied: for the release of

The Simpson's Movie, the company converted 12 of its North American stores into the show's Kwik-E-Marts, selling special products based on its television doppelgänger.

HIS STORY

For generations, 7-Eleven has been America's shared 24-hour hub for life's necessities. The construction worker heading to the job site before dawn stops there to get his coffee, as does the stockbroker heading into the office early. The secretary comes by in the afternoon to buy a wad of lottery tickets, passing the indomitable third-shift factory worker who's there to grab some milk and bread on her way home. The police officer makes a pit stop in the middle of the night, alongside the teenagers looking for munchies after a late movie. And on Christmas Day, when there's nowhere else open, it's where every American goes for the batteries that weren't included.

Adding to the firm's status as a national institution is that 7-Eleven has become a well-trodden path for immigrants to achieve the American dream. Whether it's the recently arrived sales clerk working the overnight shift, who in some areas is putting more than his sleep quota at risk, or the first-generation entrepreneur who uses the business as the foundation for his extended family's economic success, immigrants have played a starring role in the 7-Eleven story.

Joe DePinto's part in this story is to energize the iconic firm, positioning it to succeed in an ever changing retail landscape. A native Chicagoan raised in a blue-collar family, Joe attended West Point and graduated with a degree in engineering management. After serving in the military, Joe returned to college to get his MBA at Northwestern's prestigious Kellogg Graduate School of Management. That combination of credentials made him an attractive commodity for the corporate world, and so Joe found himself on a corporate ladder he never envisioned. Married, with four sons, Joe had stints in PepsiCo's Restaurant Division and Thornton Oil before joining 7-Eleven, where he rose to become head of operations. He briefly left to become president of GameStop, the video game and entertainment software retailer, but was brought back to 7-Eleven less than a year later to take the helm of the firm and position it for the future. "I left what I thought was a great opportunity for a job that was really difficult to pass up."

In response to the slumping economy worldwide, Joe has been trying to expand 7-Eleven's image beyond that of just offering convenience. Taking a lesson from its Japanese stores, 7-Elevens around the globe are devoting more space to fresh foods. In an effort to emphasize their roles as "neighborhood stores," domestic outlets are offering more regional and ethnic products. To provide more affordable offerings, the company has added value products sold under its new house brand, 7-Select. All these efforts don't mean that the company is ignoring its core customers: young males. Big Gulps, Slurpees, and Big Bite hot dogs are now joined by video game and movie rentals, and prepaid phones and phone cards. Joe is also trying to streamline logistics to make the giant retail network more nimble.

"I believe that to lead, you have to serve. Our job on the corporate side is to work alongside and support the folks who are taking care of customers every day."

As if this weren't enough of an agenda, Joe has also been working on changing the corporate culture of 7-Eleven. "I believe that to lead, you have to serve. Our job on the corporate side is to work alongside and support the folks who are taking care of customers every day. The transactions take place at the cash register, not at the headquarters building." That message is conveyed through words and deeds: the main corporate office is now called the "store support center" rather than "headquarters," and Joe regularly visits stores and facilities. His constant travel would have made going undercover problematic if he didn't have more than 6,000 domestic locations to choose from.

Confident in his familiarity with the environment in the chain's stores, Joe didn't approach his undercover mission as just a fact-finding expedition. "Sure, I was looking to see what we weren't doing well so we could correct those things and be better in the long run. But I also wanted to get the message out about the changes we've made and the culture we've created." And for Joe, the target audience for the message included the whole 7-Eleven team, as well as the general public. "Ultimately, I saw this as an opportunity for us to spread the word about what makes us tick and about the servant leadership approach we're trying to build."

He found a perfect, albeit unconventional example of that kind of approach to service on his first undercover assignment.

JOB #1

The Secret to a Great Cup of Coffee
Sales Associate, 7-Eleven Store #19131, Shirley NY

Coffee has been an enormous part of 7-Eleven's business for almost 50 years. It was the first retailer to sell fresh-brewed coffee to go, introducing the innovation in its Northeast stores in 1964. The company now sells over a million cups of coffee a day. Joe's first undercover assignment was at the company's store in Shirley, New York: the epicenter for coffee for 7-Eleven because it sells more than 2,500 cups of coffee a day, an extraordinary amount, and the most of any store in the system.

Joe would be working his shift with Dolores, who handles the coffee counter for the shop. A short, blunt woman in her mid-60s, Dolores has been working the morning coffee rush for more than 18 years, at two different franchised locations, each managed by a different one of her sons, and both owned by her son-in-law.

As the sun came up and the customers began trickling in, Dolores gave Joe a quick course in preparing and refreshing the coffee bar. But the lesson was interrupted when the trickle turned into a steady stream and finally a torrent of coffee buyers. Struggling to keep up, and realizing how much water they needed and how quickly things got messy, Joe suggested (he thought helpfully) that having a sink located at the coffee counter would make life easier. Dolores laughed at her trainee's "pipe dream," joking that "already he's coming up with new ideas." More stunning

than the sheer number of customers was that Dolores seemed to have a personal relationship with each, greeting him or her by name and exchanging in the kind of teasing quick back-and-forth that substitutes for morning conversation in metro New York.

Joe met one customer who said she'd been friendly with Dolores for 20 years. The woman revealed that Dolores had only one kidney and went for dialysis twice a week. She refused to accept a donated kidney from any of her children for fear that they might get sick themselves one day and need that spare organ. When Joe asked Dolores about it, she didn't minimize the problem, but neither did she accept credit for being anyone special.

Joe, in contrast, did realize how special Dolores was, and how much her personality drove the store's success. "They're selling 2,500 cups of coffee there, not because they have great coffee, but because they have Dolores. We're always talking about our locations as being neighborhood stores and providing customer service. Well, Dolores epitomizes that. She cares about her customers like they're part of her family. Dolores knows their names and what's going on in their lives. That kind of personal touch is powerful whether it takes place during a two-hour-long visit to a high-end department store or during a hurried two-minute visit to grab a cup of coffee on your way to work."

JOB #2

The Donut Detail

Line Operator, 7-Eleven Bakery, Baltimore MD

More than 60 million pastries a year are made in 7-Eleven's bakeries. Those facilities, and the company's network of commissaries, play a big role in Joe's future plans. "Our organization is really

trying to expand freshly made foods in our stores, and bakery items are key." That's why Joe decided to spend his second day undercover at the company's largest bakery, located in Baltimore.

Joe's boss for the day was Phil, 48, a baker and dough maker at the plant for eight years, who also served as the head of trainees. A Marine Corps veteran who retired after 12 years of service, Phil joked that he found his job by following the smell of doughnuts. Phil gave Joe an overview of some of the active machines at the plant, finally stationing him at the line where raw fritters were placed on belts to be sent into the fryers. Joe had difficulty filling each belt with the required five fritters without getting help from Phil or another employee. Joe's undercover glasses kept sliding down his nose, forcing him to push them back with his flour-coated hands. Whether he kept missing spots due to his poor technique or not being able to see through flour-covered lenses wasn't clear.

The two men soon realized they had much in common and were bonding over their shared military experiences. Combining good-natured jabs with some tips for how he could keep up with the speeding belt, Phil eventually coached Joe so that the recruit could at least pull his own weight. It seemed that if he got a strap to hold his eyeglasses tight, he might even have a productive career at the bakery.

During a break, Phil showed Joe his artwork, which he created in his spare time. An accomplished illustrator, Phil hoped to start his own freelance graphic arts business at some point. Phil did a quick sketch of a doughnut to commemorate Joe's first shift, and the two ex-military men toasted each other with doughnuts.

Unlike most of the undercover bosses who worked factory line positions, Joe seemed to enjoy himself. "It was great," he stressed. "There was no corporate talk or anything like that. It was making doughnuts and having fun." Part of his comfort also came from the confidence he gained about the future of the factory. "The facility was operating extremely well . . . until I got on the line and slowed them up. Phil's background as a sergeant in the Marines and his sense of humor make him a great trainer. Having him in charge of training at that unit really set my mind at ease. I knew he'd make sure the products coming out of that bakery would measure up to the high standards we have."

"It was great. There was no corporate talk or anything like that. It was making doughnuts and having fun."

PRODUCERS' NOTE
What You Didn't See

During the 7-Eleven episode, one of our talented crew members received some recognition for his impressive work. While filming Joe giving his reactions to the process so far, Roger Ross Williams, the episode's director, heard his phone begin to ring. We watched in confusion as he interrupted the shoot to reach into his pocket and take the call. But before any of us had time to chastise Roger for his momentary lapse in professionalism, he let out an excited shriek and exclaimed, barely able to speak, "I've just been nominated for an Oscar!" His short film, "Music by Prudence," went on to capture the award for Best Documentary, Short Subject.

JOB #3

No Future

Overnight Sales Associate, 7-Eleven Store #32211, Medford NY

Being open 24 hours a day has been one of the keys to the success of 7-Eleven. As America increasingly moves to an around-the-clock business schedule, 7-Eleven needs to ensure that it can maintain its always-open policy. "The difference between working the morning coffee rush and working the third shift is like the difference between night and day," Joe joked. "It's not just the pace and the velocity of the work, it's also the duties and responsibilities involved."

Arriving for his overnight shift at 11 P.M., Joe was met by Waqas, 26, who'd be his boss for the night. Waqas emigrated from Pakistan to the United States seven years prior and had worked nights at 7-Eleven for four years. In that time he became the franchise manager's go-to clerk, willing to do whatever was asked of him.

Assigned to do general cleanup and stocking, Joe swept the parking lot and restocked shelves, and soon was standing around, yawning, looking for something to do. Waqas obliged, having Joe clean the bathrooms and take out the trash. Restocking the prepared sandwiches after a delivery, Waqas and Joe had a chance to talk. Joe learned that Waqas worked the night shift because it made it easier for him to attend college during the day. He was working toward his bachelor's degree in criminal justice.

As the morning neared and fresh-baked goods arrived for the morning rush, Waqas had Joe help him throw out all the unsold doughnuts, rolls, muffins, and bagels. Joe was surprised but, though upset, kept his cool and his cover. "7-Eleven has a Harvest Program for perishable food items to go to charities rather than being thrown in the garbage. I knew Waqas was just following directions, but it was frustrating for me to see so much food go to waste. We have 6,500 stores in the U.S. That's a lot of food that can go to hungry people. It's something I'm passionate about, and I knew that I had to get fixed."

Later investigating the issue of wasted food, Joe learned that the store management had overordered baked goods that day, eager for the store to look its best for the camera crew they knew would be arriving (for what they had been told was a documentary on entry-level jobs). He also discovered that many of the larger nonprofit organizations won't accept unpackaged food, such as donuts and rolls. "We've learned that our team has to make more grassroots efforts to work with local organizations to find ways to cut through bureaucracy and develop solutions to meet the needs of those in the community. We're a company of neighborhood stores, so that kind of approach is a perfect fit."

In the midst of their shift, Waqas's father brought his son's lunch, which Waqas had forgotten, as well as his own. There was enough for three, and because Joe was a guest, Waqas invited him to share their meal. Sitting in the storeroom at a makeshift table made of cardboard cartons, Joe asked Waqas how he felt about the company. Waqas confessed that he thought there was no future for him in the company because there was no way for him to advance. "I wouldn't recommend anyone come to work for 7-Eleven," he added, "since there's no room for you to grow."

"Great people make great companies, and we can't let them think their job's a dead end. We can't win the battle without great soldiers."

Joe had been upset about the wasted food, but what really disappointed him were Waqas's feelings about his company. "It hurt that Waqas, who's this great, hardworking young man, didn't believe he had an opportunity with 7-Eleven. Great people make great companies, and we can't let them think their job's a dead end. We can't win the battle without great soldiers."

Joe didn't see Waqas's working for a franchisee, not 7-Eleven itself, as any excuse. "We help our franchisees recruit for their stores. Likewise, we encourage our franchisees to help us on the corporate side find great people. We've had corporate people become operators and operators become corporate people. Ultimately, if there's a person, like Waqas, who has the talent to do other things and wants to do more, but isn't given the opportunity, they'll end up leaving the organization. And that's a loss for both the franchisee and the company. I needed to send the message to all our team members that there are opportunities for people to grow at 7-Eleven."

JOB #4

A Failure to Communicate

Store Manager, 7-Eleven Store #23754, Southampton NY

Joe's next undercover assignment took him to one of the highest-grossing of the 36,000 stores in the 7-Eleven system. His goal was to see how well such a busy store and the support center in Dallas worked together.

Lorie, the store manager, put Joe to work right away, assigning him to clean the front doors of the open, active store. Working around the dozens of customers who came in and out the door, Joe managed to clean them thoroughly, only to be told by Lorie that they'd be covered with fingerprints again in 10 minutes. With a laugh and a shrug, she explained, "We do the best that we can." Joe did general floor duties for most of the morning, restocking shelves, refreshing the fresh foods, and sweeping up. Then Lorie asked him to handle a maintenance call for her.

The support center in Dallas is responsible for maintaining the stores for the franchisees. When there's a problem, the franchisee calls in, and headquarters sends out a team to take care of it. There were a number of lights out on the store's selling floor, and lights in the storage room were out, so Lorie asked Joe to call in and arrange for a maintenance team to come fix them. After calling in the problem, Joe was shocked to learn that it was assigned a low priority and wouldn't be addressed until the next regularly scheduled maintenance visit a month later.

Joe was stunned by the system's lack of responsiveness to situations that had a direct impact on customers and safety. He excused himself, called the company's chief operating officer from his car, and arranged for the lights to be replaced immediately. Although he wasn't happy that the system had let down even one of the network's highest-grossing stores, Joe was gratified he'd discovered the situation and could work at correcting the problem. "We really need to do everything we can to support our stores. It's important to me, and it's vital for the future of our company. That was just the kind of situation that we want to hear from our franchisees about. When I got back to Dallas, I sat down with our facilities team, and we went over the various maintenance issues and made changes to the system so those that affect the customer directly or impact safety all now have a high priority."

> "We really need to do everything we can to support our stores. It's important to me, and it's vital for the future of our company."

JOB #5

The American Dream

Delivery Truck Driver, 7-Eleven Combined Distribution Center, Lewisville TX

For his final undercover assignment, Joe flew home to Texas to work at one of the company's distribution centers. "The distribution folks are the unsung heroes of the company. The customer has no idea of all the work that goes into getting products to the stores. Their jobs are critically important, and I'm looking forward to spending time with them."

Joe would be spending his shift with Igor, 48. Igor emigrated from Kazakhstan 15 years ago, arriving with a wife, two children, and $50 in his pocket. Despite leaving behind a life as a college-educated officer in the Russian military, Igor loves the job he's held for the past 10 years: driving a delivery truck for 7-Eleven. Explaining that he loved his truck and would hug it if his arms were long enough, Igor enlisted Joe's help in loading it with the evening's deliveries. At 10 P.M. they set out on their route of 13 stores.

Igor's humor and enthusiasm were infectious as he led Joe from store to store, introducing him by name to all the night clerks on the route. It was obvious that Igor's visit was more than just a resupply mission for the stores; it was a morale boost. When Joe asked Igor if he missed his family, having to work the night shift, Igor explained that it gave him and his wife less time to argue, and that because they had less time to spend together, they were more affectionate and attentive.

Joe's pleasure at working with the personable and enthusiastic Igor was shaken when he learned that the next stop on their route would be the 7-Eleven closest to Joe's home. "I go into that store all the time," Joe explained. "Everyone there knows me, including the franchise owner." After helping Igor unload the truck, Joe spotted that franchise owner in the store. Trying to ensure that his cover wouldn't be blown, Joe told Igor he had to use the bathroom around the back of the gas station, where he hid for the entire visit, letting Igor handle the delivery himself.

As they went through the rest of the route, Joe was compelled to ask Igor how he stayed so motivated, working through the night in all sorts of weather, all year long. "I'm living the American dream," he declared. "America is the best country in the world. You guys don't know how blessed you are. This isn't a story about me; it's a story about America. I came here with no English, no knowledge of the culture, 50 bucks in my pocket. I'm blessed. You ask why I'm so motivated? Because I'm so thankful for this country that has allowed me to survive and be happy."

"To see folks working as hard as they were made me feel great as a CEO. They made me want to work even harder to ensure we're giving them all we can to support them in what they do."

Igor's love for his adopted country was just the icing on the cake for Joe, who in the past week had seen nothing but extraordinary employees, and whose only negative discoveries were corporate failures to deliver what his people needed. "I've always been someone who's very committed to the business. To see folks working as hard as they were made me feel great as a CEO. They made me want to work even harder to ensure we're giving them all we can to support them in what they do."

HE REVEALS THE TRUTH

"We've got more work to do." That was the message Joe delivered to his executive committee when he met with them on his return to headquarters. "Everyone knows we have a program where we give away sandwiches and bakery items to charities. But in one store I was in, we threw those products away. Then there was the experience I had where lights were out in the store, and they couldn't get them repaired right away. We've addressed both those specific situations, but we have to always zero in on what the stores' issues are and put the fixes in place. Every single employee I met was amazing. What we have to do is support them better."

"Every single employee I met was amazing. What we have to do is support them better."

Next, Joe met with all the people he'd worked with during his undercover week, who'd been brought to headquarters not knowing what was in store for them.

Waqas, the young student working behind the counter, didn't recognize "Danny" when Joe entered. Explaining how impressed he was with Waqas's efforts to get his education while working the night shift, and how upset he was that Waqas didn't feel he had any room to grow at 7-Eleven, Joe said that whether the young man wanted to return to Pakistan and help

PRODUCERS' NOTE
What You Didn't See

Lorie was unable to attend the taping of the reveal, but Joe was extremely impressed with Lorie and the way she ran her store. In order to best utilize her leadership skills and get more stores running as well as Lorie's, Joe gave Lorie a spot on the 7-Eleven's Franchise Leadership Advisory Council. This organization meets quarterly to give franchisees a voice in management issues and allows them to discuss changes in the general market-place. Lorie was thrilled and flattered to be offered the opportunity to represent Long Island franchisees, and promised always to give the council the straight story about what's happening on the front lines.

his country, or stay in America, Joe and the company would be there to help. "I will personally look after you as a mentor, and I'll try to help you succeed either here at 7-Eleven or if you decide to go back to your country." Waqas was overjoyed at the prospects, noting that "I feel more confident that I'll be successful in my life."

When Joe revealed his true identity to Phil, all the ex-Marine could say was "Get out of Dodge!" Saying how much he enjoyed working with Phil, and how much he appreciated the way the trainer picked up his slack, Joe told Phil that he'd have the opportunity to do some freelance art for the company's advertising agency, to build up his portfolio. "It's a dream coming true for me," Phil confessed.

Joe told Dolores that he had discovered customers weren't coming to 7-Eleven in record numbers just because of the coffee, they were coming because of her. He said the company wanted to do what it could to help her overcome her health issues. "We're going to set up a Dolores Donor Awareness program to encourage our employees and franchises across the United States and Canada to get involved and remind people how important it is to fill out an organ donor card." Dolores was thrilled by the gesture. "Oh my God, that's just wonderful. I love it. God bless you for that."

Igor immediately recognized his helper, but was stunned when he learned his true identity. Joe said that in recognition of all Igor's hard work and dedication, he was going to send the driver and his wife on a nice vacation so they could spend some quality time together. "Big boss comes to plain worker. I could not believe what had happened. Only in a movie. Only in a book. Only in America."

Still reveling in the joy of being able to help those with whom he'd worked, Joe addressed a crowd of staff and franchisees who'd been brought to headquarters for the occasion. After sharing video clips of his experiences, Joe spoke from the heart. "I thought I knew our stores. The fact is, I have a lot more to learn, and you all taught me that. You'll be seeing me and our team working with you to find out what your challenges are, so that we can all collectively better serve our

"The fact is, I have a lot more to learn, and you all taught me that. You'll be seeing me and our team working with you to find out what your challenges are, so that we can all collectively better serve our customers. That's my commitment to you."

customers. That's my commitment to you. This will change the way I work every day as CEO of our company."

Subsequently appearing on an episode of the *Oprah Winfrey Show* that looked at the *Undercover Boss* phenomenon, Joe had some additional surprises for Dolores and Igor. He presented Dolores with season tickets to her beloved New York Yankees. Most dramatically, he told Igor that his hard work, unstinting enthusiasm, and unbridled love for America were so inspiring that 7-Eleven wanted to do more than just send him on a vacation. Joe announced that the company was waiving its usual franchise fee and presenting Igor with his own store.

However much the convenience store business changes, and whatever global best practices are imported into its stores, 7-Eleven will remain the most American of businesses. Not just because of its focus on convenience. Not only because it sells Slurpees, Big Gulps, and Big Bites. And not solely because it's a nearly ubiquitous presence on the landscape, frequented by a cross section of the population. 7-Eleven is the quintessential American business because it also provides immigrants with the chance to become full-fledged members of the culture, as well as the opportunity to carve out a financially secure path for themselves and their families. "We say that the 7-Eleven sign is also the sign of opportunity," Joe recalled. "Being able to offer thousands of people a pathway to their American Dream is part of our corporate DNA."

SINCE THE SHOW

★ **Waqas** has been provided with the path for growth he didn't think was available. He is training to become a field consultant for 7-Eleven, responsible for 10 franchise stores.

★ **Phil** has been hired as a freelance illustrator by 7-Eleven's advertising agency and is using the opportunity to build up his portfolio.

★ Inspired by **Dolores**, 7-Eleven has set up a donor awareness program. The company has also donated $150,000 to a kidney foundation in Dolores's honor. And Joe has made his pipe dream real and arranged for a sink to be installed in that store's coffee counter.

★ **Lorie** was ecstatic that her maintenance issues were addressed so quickly and that Joe prompted a review of the way repair issues were prioritized. Joe invited her to join the company's newly formed National Business Leadership Council, and Lorie has become an active participant in that group's Customer Experience subcommittee.

★ **Igor** is now his own boss. His 7-Eleven franchise was opened in Richardson, Texas, in May 2010. Joe was there for the first day of business and the store's grand opening.

★ Although all the employees he worked with touched **Joe** in some way, the stories of Waqas and Igor had particular and lasting resonance for the West Point graduate. "America is a country built on immigrants and entrepreneurs. We at 7-Eleven have been fortunate to be able to give many of these individuals an opportunity to work in our stores. I can't tell you how many of these people have risen in our organization to become franchisees and give back to their communities. I'm proud that our organization has provided these kinds of opportunities to deserving people."

AN AMERICAN LOVE AFFAIR

"White Castle isn't just a job to me. It's my life. It's my family's life."

David Rife
Owner, White Castle

David Allen
Job Seeker

How We Found the Boss

America's love affair with the hamburger may well have started with White Castle, the country's first burger chain. So when we had a craving for a quick-service food company to feature in our first season, we headed for the castle. White Castle is family owned and managed, and we had the pleasure of meeting several members of the fourth generation. White Castle executive Jamie Richardson was our host as we toured various facilities across Ohio, with a mandatory stop at corporate headquarters (lovingly referred to by one awestruck employee as "the White Castle Pentagon"). Dave Rife, the oldest member of the fourth generation, agreed to go undercover and share his findings with his siblings and close family on the executive committee.

THE BOSS

David Rife, family member–owner and plant manager of White Castle's porcelain steel building division.

HIS COVER

David Allen, an employee of a heavy equipment company who has been laid off, and who's being filmed for a television show about people trying out entry-level jobs.

HIS COMPANY

Founded in Wichita, Kansas, in 1921 by Walter Anderson and Edgar W. "Billy" Ingram, White Castle is credited as the first fast-food restaurant. With these small, stand-alone restaurants, the founders set out to create a pristine, inexpensive dining experience. The restaurants were designed to resemble miniature castles, complete with buttresses and crenellated towers. White Castle invented many of the processes that are now common practice in the fast-food industry, including being the first to standardize food preparation methods, ensuring uniformity for customers and turning the cook into "an infinitely replaceable technician." The White Castle founders did for burgers what Henry Ford had done for cars. The small square hamburgers called (and now trademarked) "Sliders" were priced at five cents each well into the 1940s. Billy Ingram bought out Anderson in 1933, and moved the headquarters to Columbus, Ohio. The company built up its own infrastructure with bakeries, meat supply plants, and warehouses, and spun off separate businesses from its paper hat and porcelain steel building divisions. There are now 421 Castles in 11 primarily midwestern states, though there is a sizable long-standing cluster in the metropolitan New York area. Most of the company's restaurants are open 24 hours a day. The chain's comparatively small size hasn't hurt profitability. White Castle ranks number two in the fast-food industry for sales revenue per store, trailing only McDonald's, which has more than 13,000 outlets in the United States.

HIS STORY

Every family has legacies, some by design and some by default. These can be anything from a calling to public service, as with the Kennedys, to passed down traditional holiday recipes; as spiritual as a shared faith or as tangible as a shared fortune. Legacies can be gifts or burdens—sometimes a little of both. But they always come with an implicit responsibility toward the next generation, either to preserve and strengthen a generational thread that's beneficial or to sever one that's harmful. David Rife bears both these responsibilities.

Almost 90 years after its founding, White Castle System, as the company is formally known, remains a family-owned business, with each of its restaurants company owned rather than franchised, which is common with other chains. Founder Billy Ingram was determined that the company remain in private hands and refrain from taking on debt. He was replaced by his son E. W. Ingram Jr., who was in turn replaced by *his* son E. W. Ingram III. Today there are four remaining third-generation family members, all of whom own and work in the business. Next in line are 17 fourth-generation family members, nine of whom currently own and work in the business. And waiting in the wings are 26 fifth-generation family members. Dave, a great-grandson of the founder, and member of the company's executive council, is the oldest and de facto leader of the fourth generation of family member–owners.

White Castle's unique ownership structure and conservative business philosophy have led to its remaining largely a regional business. But in some ways, the company's small footprint has contributed to its perennial appeal and cultlike following. The company calls its devoted fans "Cravers." In 2001, in honor of the company's 80th anniversary, White Castle created a Cravers Hall of Fame, and began inducting a handful of nominees each year. To meet the needs of its devotees who don't live near a restaurant, White Castle sells boxes of frozen hamburgers in grocery stores nationwide. In recent years, White Castle has gained additional attention for its Valentine's Day tradition of taking reservations for candlelit tables for two, complete with formally dressed table servers.

The company's traditional, family-oriented business approach extends to its employees. The "extended family" workforce is unusually loyal and has a very low turnover rate for the fast-food industry. There are many employees with more than 20 years of service. One employee recently retired after 67 years with the company. "My great-grandfather started this company with some core principles: integrity, honesty, and job security," Dave explains. "He believed our people are the most important asset we have. There's a stereotype in America about the entry-level person—in our industry it's the proverbial burger

> "The burger flipper and every other entry-level person is too often overlooked and underappreciated. These are hardworking Americans whose jobs aren't easy, but they do their best to give great service and provide an outstanding product every single day."

flipper. Well, the burger flipper and every other entry-level person is too often overlooked and underappreciated. These are hardworking Americans whose jobs aren't easy, but they do their best to give great service and provide an outstanding product every single day."

A trim, athletic man in his mid-40s, married with two grown sons, Dave has spent 20 years rising through the company's ranks, working in restaurant operations, engineering, construction, and manufacturing at various points. With his goatee and red Corvette, Dave is one of the more colorful family members. "Being part of the family that owns White Castle has enabled me to have a pretty nice lifestyle—I've got a lot of toys." Despite Dave's flamboyance, his working life is driven by a very traditional goal: to ensure that family ownership and the company's approach continue not just into the fifth generation but to the sixth and beyond.

Up until recently, however, it didn't look as though Dave would be around to see the next generation come into its patrimony. "If I hadn't changed some of my habits, I'd probably not have been around very long. At my heaviest I weighed 271 pounds. I had high blood pressure and high cholesterol. I was a heart attack waiting to happen." One day Dave just decided it was time to make a change. He started exercising regularly and dramatically changed his eating habits. He now avoids even his own company's fried foods, sticking to its famously steam-grilled Sliders. Over a two-year period, Dave underwent a physical metamorphosis, dropping so much weight that he now looks completely different. "I think I saved my life," he admits.

He also provided himself with a ready disguise. Besides a 75-pound weight loss, Dave agreed to sacrifice his goatee for the success of an undercover mission to ensure that his family's legacy is passed on to the next generation of family members and employees. "White Castle isn't just a job to me. It's my life. It's my family's life."

Despite Dave's enthusiasm and dedication, there was some doubt among the rest of the family. Some of his more conservative relatives found the idea of an owner going undercover while being followed by a television crew a bit far outside the box. There were also those, including Dave's own brother Brad, who expressed misgivings about Dave's being able to do the work required, frontline work he hadn't done since he was a teenager. "It may take me a while," Dave conceded. "But then again, it shouldn't look like I've been doing this every day." It would turn out that Dave needn't have worried about appearing too proficient.

JOB #1

Too Many Cooks

Team Member, White Castle Restaurant, Hamilton OH

White Castle opens 10 to 12 new restaurants every year, each of which, for a private company of its size, represents a huge investment of time and money. During the first few weeks of operation at a new location, the company floods the restaurant with staff, bringing over team members from existing locations in addition to those newly hired. Dave was being added to this mix at a newly opened White Castle.

Geenie, the general manager of the new store, issued Dave his uniform and then handed him off to the kitchen team. Dave

found himself caught in a confused mob. The kitchen, a narrow space to begin with, was teeming with employees—two or three to each one-man job—and soon people were crashing into each other or, worse, standing around bored, watching. Further lending to the chaos, multiple managers were telling multiple people what to do and where to go, even contradicting one another. Geenie obviously wasn't pleased with the situation. Pointing to the group of seemingly bored employees manning the front counter, Genie asked David, "Do they look like they're enjoying their jobs?" With team members not knowing what to do, or not having anything to do, morale clearly suffered.

In an effort to, as much as anything, keep Dave from being trampled, Geenie assigned him his own personal guide, Donna, a 50-year-old veteran of the company. Donna spent the next few hours training Dave on various kitchen and counter duties, shifting from station to station whenever the crowd in any one area thinned out. Breaking for lunch, Dave selected a couple of

Sliders, but turned down the offers of anything fried. Impressed by his will power, Donna confessed her own lack of self-denial. "I had a heart attack in 2003 and almost died. I love to eat all the things I shouldn't. My husband is on disability and he always tells me that he doesn't know what he'd do if something happened to me. I want to live a long time, but the way I'm going, I know I won't."

Dave's first day had been productive but unsettling. "It's obvious the extra help did more harm than good. There's a disconnect between the home office and the people in the field on this issue. They know what they need. We have to do a better

PRODUCERS' NOTE
What You Didn't See

Dave and Donna immediately connected over the similarity of their health problems. We saw that Donna inspired the boss to set up a wellness program for White Castle team members, but what we didn't see was how Dave began personally motivating Donna from the moment they met. As soon as he finished filming his immediate reactions about his time in the Hamilton store, Dave turned around and marched right back inside. He found Donna, gave her his phone number, and assured her that she could call him any time for support. Maintaining his character, Dave told a visibly emotional Donna that if he got a job at White Castle, he would happily go on walks with her, share his own experiences, and become an essential motivating force for Donna's weight-loss journey.

Dave kept in touch with Donna—still in his undercover persona—all the way up until the finale, where she found out the true identity of her undercover supporter.

job of listening." But it wasn't just procedural changes Dave knew he needed to initiate. "Donna survived a heart attack that most people don't. I was at that point a couple of years ago. If I hadn't made the kind of changes in my lifestyle I did, I might not be here. If I found out Donna had a heart attack two months from now, I'd have a lot of guilt." Dave knew he wanted to do something to help her and all his staff who struggled with weight issues.

JOB #2

Good Day for Hogs

Team Member, White Castle Bakery, Rensselaer IN

Believing that the best way to ensure that his restaurants served quality products was to control as many variables as possible, White Castle founder Billy Ingram strove to make the company self-reliant. A famous quip was that the only things White Castle didn't do for itself were raise the cows and grow the wheat. Although Dave had spent most of his career in these support businesses, he'd never worked in the bakery, so he looked forward to his assignment there, even though it was on the night shift.

Steve, the imposing production supervisor, led Dave on a quick introductory tour of the bakery, his voice raised so that they could communicate over the roar of the machinery. After proudly explaining the incredible volume of production generated daily, Steve set Dave up at the bagging station. The complex array of equipment stacked together four sheets, each with 30 buns, and then pushed the assembled pile into a cardboard box.

Dave's job was to hold a plastic bag in position so that the mass of buns would be slid into the bag just before it was pushed into the box. Steve warned Dave to keep his hands away from the paddle that guided the rolls "because it will come down and take the skin right off your arm."

Duly warned, but confident, Dave took command. His first effort was a failure, as the trailing edge of the pile of buns was crushed against the opening of the carton. Steve patiently showed Dave how to shut down the machine, remove the crushed buns, and restart the process. Undaunted, Dave tried it again. This time half the top sheet of rolls missed the box entirely. Steve once again shut down the machine and cleared it. Dave kept trying, Steve kept clearing, and the wasted rolls kept piling up. Dave's competitive fire and frustration took over, and he became locked in a battle of wills with the machine. He was like a boxer refusing to give up even though clearly outmatched. Someone was going to have to stop Dave before he hurt himself or bankrupted his family's business. Mercifully, Steve threw in the towel and declared the machine the winner.

"People don't expect the boss to be able to outpace or outwork them, but they do want the boss to be competent enough to do their job. I know that it's okay for people to make mistakes . . . it's just that I didn't apply that to myself."

Totaling up the damage, Steve explained to Dave that he had smashed 20 to 25 cases. Trying to find a bright side, he told Dave that his efforts wouldn't go to waste. "All of our waste is loaded in barrels, and a hog farmer comes and picks them up and feeds them to his animals. You fed the pigs really well this week."

Being a porcine benefactor wasn't of much comfort to Dave. He was so upset that he called home and woke his wife so that she could talk him off the ledge. "I always tried to make sure that whatever I was doing was just one step above so I wouldn't disappoint my family. I wanted them to be proud of me, and I wanted everybody in the company to be proud of me. People don't expect the boss to be able to outpace or outwork them, but they do want the boss to be competent enough to do their job. I know that it's okay for people to make mistakes . . . it's just that I didn't apply that to myself."

JOB #3

Fear and Joy on the Late Shift

Team Member, White Castle Restaurant, Covington KY

Eager to put his hog-feeding experience behind him, Dave next went to work a night shift at a long established Castle in Covington, Kentucky. Although the company has historically kept most White Castle restaurants open 24 hours a day, it was in the process of reevaluating the policy.

Tina, the assistant general manager of the restaurant, welcomed Dave and led him back to meet Darlene, the chef manager, who showed him how to work the grill. Darlene coached Dave on the procedure for assembling a Slider—an exacting process with its own handbook, rules, and order of ingredients—pointing out some minor modifications to the process they'd come up with in the restaurant to streamline the procedure. Tina, who had been standing nearby, leaned in and with obvious concern, warned Dave not to pick up bad habits like straying in any way from the exact procedure.

During a break, Tina explained her earlier caution. "Bad habits can get you fired," she warned. "Follow White Castle procedures exactly. Lay out your grill the right way. Don't over-stuff your fryer. If they come in and catch you doing something not by the book, they have the authority to fire you right then and there." Tina confessed that she came in every day worrying she'd get fired.

As the evening continued, the pace in the shop picked up, and Dave was assigned to work the drive-through window with Joe. The lighthearted 30-year-old told Dave he worked at five different restaurants and on various shifts. Joe was less obsessed with procedure than with providing excellent customer service. "You don't have to be formal and say things exactly the same way, as long as you're polite and friendly." Joe demonstrated

how to personally engage with each customer, while still getting the complicated job done efficiently. Taking a break when the late-night rush slowed down, Dave pressed Joe for his secret. Joe thought he was such an accomplished communicator because he had a visually impaired son and spent much of his time at home talking. He deflected Dave's praise for his positive personality. "I depend on this job to take care of my family. That's why I work so hard at it."

Dave came away from his late-night experience with mixed feelings; he was upset by Tina's fears, but bolstered by Joe's enthusiasm. "The procedures we've created at the home office are intended for the *benefit* of our team members and to ensure our customers get a uniform product every time. Having been born into this family, I've never had to worry about my job," he admitted. "But one of the core principles my great-grandfather built this company on was job security, not just for the family, but for our team members too. If Tina is afraid for her job every day, that's our fault." As troubling as that discovery was, finding Joe was inspiring. "He has an attitude that pulled people up and motivated them. We have to do something more to help him fully utilize his skills."

JOB #4

Culinary Dreams

Team Member, White Castle Restaurant, Chicago IL

With an eye toward a future in which his generation would eventually be leading the business, Dave was interested in working with younger employees to get a sense for how well the company was doing in providing them with opportunities. As a result he'd been sent to Chicago to work with Jose, 17, who'd started working for White Castle at 16, on the first day he could legally be hired. A first-generation Mexican American, Jose had become a standout performer at the restaurant.

Following and assisting the diligent Jose as he restocked the cooking area, unloaded deliveries into the freezers, and took out the trash, Dave was struck by the young man's energy and drive. The personable teen opened up to Dave, revealing that his dream was to become a chef and open his own restaurant. He confessed that he didn't think there were any opportunities for him at White Castle. When Jose and Dave took their lunch break together, Dave had a chance to sample and be dazzled by some of Jose's homemade green salsa on his Sliders. Emboldened by Dave's praise, Jose proclaimed that even though his parents didn't take his culinary dream seriously, he was going to pursue his goal even if he had to do it on his own.

JOB #5

An Unhappy Ending

Team Member, White Castle Frozen Foods Factory, Covington KY

Dave's last day undercover was spent working in the company's frozen hamburger division. A response to the company's cult-like status among its Cravers, the division is a way to get the company's product into the hands of loyal customers who don't live near any of its restaurants.

Brenda, an assistant supervisor, was Dave's boss for the day. A 16-year veteran of White Castle, she'd only recently been promoted off the line and into management. She explained to Dave that he needed to punch in five minutes before his shift. She also pointed out that he was actually already late. Duly chastened, Dave donned his hairnet and apron and was led out to the wrapping line.

Vicky, an eight-year White Castle veteran, trained Dave on how to feed the wrapping machine. She demonstrated how

 PRODUCERS' NOTE
What You Didn't See

When we visited the White Castle frozen products factory in Covington, Kentucky, we had Dave stay in a "budget" motel to enhance the experience of posing as an entry-level employee. Dave was a remarkably good sport, despite such red flags as a sign by the entryway that read NO REFUNDS AFTER 10 MINUTES. Despite the lack of linens in the room and the decidedly unhealthy odors, Dave remained in high spirits, even cracking a few jokes about the bugs climbing the walls (which he referred to as his "new roommates").

But insect infestation was the least of our worries that night. The high volume of people going in and out of Dave's room that night, including our small camera crew, attracted the attention of the local authorities. Just after we realized that the Covington Police were monitoring our comings and goings, we were surrounded by squad cars—headlights blazing—and officers asking us a barrage of questions. To make matters worse, we had to maintain the confidentiality of the show, so we couldn't even tell them what the cameras were for. Dave's official White Castle ID eventually put them at ease—but *Undercover Boss* came disturbingly close to becoming *America's Most Wanted*.

to gather two fully prepared burgers in each hand as they slid past on one slowly moving belt, and quickly push them into designated areas on a parallel faster-moving belt, without dislodging the bun or contents. The process required the dexterity of a croupier and the hand-eye coordination of a billiards champ. Dave possessed neither. Suppressing curses, Dave found his frustration growing in direct proportion to the number of destroyed Sliders that littered his work area. Dave considered it a success that he hadn't disrupted the wrapping operation the way he'd slowed down the bakery.

Chatting in the break room, Vicky revealed that morale had fallen in the eight years she'd been in the factory. Supervisors were spending more time in the break room than helping out. "The people picking up the slack are just getting more aggravated every day."

Trying to digest the discontent he'd discovered, Dave went back onto the line. He and Vicky were next assigned to work with Bonita at the cheese inspection station. Dave's job was to straighten the slices of cheese on the burgers and to add cheese to any burgers lacking a slice. Bonita backstopped Dave as he tried to get up to speed, but when the number of burgers lacking cheese started to increase, the work backed up. The three line workers scrambled to keep up and managed to help each other, though the supervisors remained on the sidelines, not offering any assistance to the increasingly overstretched line workers.

PRODUCERS' NOTE
What You Didn't See

Although Vicky talked about the feuding between the line workers and the supervisors, Dave saw some good-natured laughter in the Covington frozen products factory. After working with Vicky and Brenda, Dave learned how to apply onions to the burgers from Patty, a jovial machine operator who considers herself the joker of the factory. One way Patty tries to make the newcomers feel welcome is to entrust them with the responsibility of retrieving pickles from the second floor of the warehouse.

When Patty presented Dave with this task, he was eager to comply. However, if Dave had studied his company's product line a little closer, he would have realized that frozen White Castle burgers don't come with pickles. As he dutifully searched the facility, Dave came across another problem: he couldn't find the stairs! (The warehouse was, in fact, only one story high!) He asked everyone he could find for directions, from line workers to forklift operators, and they all laughingly sent him deeper and deeper into his wild goose chase. By the time he figured out the ruse, he was red in the face from running all across the factory—but between the beads of sweat was the unmistakable grin of a good-natured victim who can appreciate a good joke.

The poor morale at the factory and the lack of intervention or hands-on help from supervisors were just two more troubling discoveries for Dave. "Right now there are some unhappy employees at this plant." Thinking back over the overstaffing, fear, and morale issues he'd uncovered during his week in the field, Dave tried to put them in perspective. "When I started this journey, one of my goals was to do right by my great-grandfather and my grandfather. In the beginning I was pretty defensive, always looking for the positive side of things. But we're not a perfect company. I know this is the kind of information that they would want. I really believe that right now they're looking down and are very pleased with what I've just done."

HE REVEALS THE TRUTH

On his return to headquarters, Dave scheduled a meeting with the other members of the company's executive council and arranged for all the team members he'd worked with while undercover to be brought to the home office.

Dave didn't pull any punches. He described the incidents that frustrated him and indicated potential problems in the way the family was managing the business. "At the new store in Hamilton there were too many people. There were multiple managers telling our team members what to do, and no one was sure who to follow." Dave described Tina's fear of being fired for not doing something exactly by the book. "It bothered me to see one of our team members afraid of losing her job over procedural issues. I knew it would have bothered Billy, it would have bothered Edgar, and it would have bothered the rest of you too." He described the low morale he'd found at the

PRODUCERS' NOTE
What You Didn't See

Tina had a personal commitment that prevented her from attending the finale—and the subsequent one-on-one interview with the boss. Not content with having Tina wait until the episode aired to discover what she had really been a part of, Dave paid Tina a visit at her store. Accompanied by our camera crew and wearing his traditional corporate suit and tie, Dave revealed his true identity, personally assured Tina that her job was safe, and reasserted his promise to fix whatever problems were still out there.

frozen foods factory, which he attributed to insufficient supervisor training.

With his family members briefed on his experience, Dave met one-on-one with his coworkers.

"You got me," Donna laughed after learning that her trainee was actually the great-grandson of the founder. Dave reminded Donna that there were a lot of people who depend on her, and that she'd inspired him to put together a wellness program for her and all the other team members. Dabbing the corners of her eyes with a tissue, Donna said she was glad there were people like Dave in the world. "White Castle just went above and beyond to show me that they care." Not letting that praise soften his message, Dave had been keeping in touch with Donna off-camera since their first meeting (while still keeping his cover) and warned Donna that that wouldn't change. He would keep checking up on her progress and be her support system.

When Dave walked in to greet Jose, he asked if the young man recognized him. With a smile, Jose said yes, "just not with a suit and tie." Dave said he was going to introduce Jose to the culinary team at White Castle, but the company would also be providing him with a $5,000-per-year scholarship to the college of his choice, "because I believe in you and White Castle believes in you." Choking up, Jose said, "I never thought anything like this could happen to me."

"Eighty-eight years ago, my great-grandfather founded this company on the belief that happy team members make for happy customers. That still holds true today."

In his reveal to Brenda and Vicky from the frozen foods factory, Dave wanted to help them sort out their issues and, he hoped, find a way to have them work better together. He encouraged Vicky to express her frustration with the supervisors' lack of help and Brenda to explain why she thought the line workers needed to be more independent. Although there was tension between the two women, Dave's calm, evenhanded approach eased what could have been a far more difficult meeting. Explaining that Brenda needed to be prepared to step into the breach more frequently, Dave soothed the criticism by admitting that part of the problem was that Brenda hadn't received sufficient training for her move from the line to management. By the end of the meeting, the two women agreed to jointly try to repair the situation at the factory and build up teamwork.

On learning whom he'd coached at the drive-through window, Joe looked around the office and asked, "Am I being punked or something?" Ashton Kutcher didn't emerge from under the desk, and Joe began to tear up when Dave recounted what he'd learned from their time working together. "You epitomize the kind of person we want as part of our extended family. I want to create a program called Leaders of Tomorrow, have you help write the curriculum, and also be part of the first class of the program. The other

> "I feel fortunate that we're a family-owned business and not a public company because we get to make decisions based on long-term growth and what's best for our people, not short-term earnings and the bottom line."

thing we want to do is give you $5,000 towards the needs of your son." With tears rolling down his cheeks, Joe explained, "I never thought when I started at White Castle that there'd be these kind of opportunities out there for me. This will help me do a lot of things for my family that I didn't think were possible just working in White Castle."

Dave's next step was to tell the assembled family members and headquarters staff what he'd done for the past week. "When we family members go out into the field, we see the best of the best. What I wanted to learn was what life in our restaurants is really like; what do our team members experience on a day-to-day basis." His big takeaway? "Eighty-eight years ago, my great-grandfather founded this company on the belief that happy team members make for happy customers. That still holds true today. This experience has taught me it's very important to make sure we have lots of balance in our lives, and that we treat everybody with respect. If we do that, as individuals and as a company, I'm very confident that we're going to be around for another 88 years."

Dave had set out on his undercover adventure bearing the responsibility for ensuring that his family's business would continue to prosper not just for his generation, but for future generations. He'd found warning signs that there were areas in need of improvement, whether it was in changing procedures or improving training. He'd also found hopeful signs in the dedication and diligence of all the team members he'd met. But it was the willingness of his family to address problems and make sure employees are treated the way his grandfather and great-grandfather would have wished that convinced Dave the family business's future was secure.

By the end of his experience, Dave understood there was another legacy toward which he and the company bore responsibility. The company needed to help Donna overcome her legacy of an unhealthy lifestyle. It needed to help Jose overcome a legacy that threatened to place limits on his dreams. And it needed to help Joe transcend his personal and family circumstances and achieve his full potential. White Castle needed to do all this, not just because it made good business sense, but because that's what family members do for each other. "I feel fortunate that we're a family-owned business and not a public company because we get to make decisions based on long-term growth and what's best for our people, not short-term earnings and the bottom line."

SINCE THE SHOW

⭐ **Brenda** and **Vicky** are communicating and working better together. Productivity and morale at the factory have improved. "Brenda is an excellent worker who has been with us for a long time," Dave stressed. "Brenda's supervisory performance suffered, not because of her, but because we didn't train her as well as we could have about how to succeed in her new role. After getting that training, she's now doing an excellent job."

⭐ **Donna** was slated to be one of the first people able to take advantage of the new wellness program she inspired. The Southern Ohio region in which she works is the site of the pilot project, which gives all team members a chance to learn about healthier living and diet. They have their blood pressure and cholesterol levels checked free of charge. In addition, White Castle will be picking up the copayment cost for team members' routine checkups to encourage a proactive approach to health issues. However, in late May 2010, Donna's husband was hospitalized with a possible heart attack. She's currently helping him through his recovery. When he returns to health, everyone hopes Donna will be able to take care of herself as well.

⭐ **Joe** has worked with White Castle's human resource and training department to develop the company's new Leaders of Tomorrow program. The program is being designed to make sure young, talented team members realize there is a future for them at White Castle, providing them with the training, skills, and opportunities they need to work their way into the management levels of the company. Elements of the program were actually used to help Brenda improve her supervisory skills. The $5,000 gift has helped with Joe's son Jordan's education.

★ In the fall, **Jose** will be attending the Kendall College School of Culinary Arts in Chicago. In addition to the $20,000 ($5,000 per year) pledged by White Castle, the National Restaurant Association provided him with an additional $10,000 scholarship. Jose accompanied Dave and Joe when the two recently attended the National Restaurant Show in Chicago. While there, Dave introduced Jose to Rick Roman, who runs the Signature Room restaurant on the 95th floor of the Hancock Building in downtown Chicago. The restaurateur agreed to serve as Jose's mentor. White Castle is also working with Jose to develop his salsa recipe as a Slider topping.

★ **Dave** now has additional responsibilities, including leadership of the company's porcelain steel building division and, despite his lack of prowess at the bagging station, leadership of the company's three bakeries and three meat plants. Looking back, Dave believes that although a certain amount of disconnect between the corner office and the front line is inevitable, it can be minimized. One way they're trying to do that at White Castle is that, in honor of National Hamburger Month (May), everyone at the company's home office is encouraged to work one shift in a restaurant to better understand and appreciate what frontline people go through on a daily basis. "Any executive who has a chance to go undercover in their organization shouldn't hesitate. If you go into it with an open mind and are willing to face the tougher side as well as the good side of it, you and your company can only grown and improve.

"On a personal level, the experience taught me to better open my eyes, my ears, and my heart and absorb everything I can from other people, no matter who they are or what their job or profession is," Dave added. "There is so much out there you can learn from people, if you're open to it. Something might seem inconsequential when you hear it today, but tomorrow, in a different context, it could be revelatory. It's easy to sit behind a desk and make decisions based on numbers. Now, every time I look at those numbers, I'm going to put a face to them, and try to think about how the decisions I make will impact those faces."

There's been one more personal change. At the urging of his wife, Dave has remained clean shaven.

> "There is so much out there you can learn from people, if you're open to it. Something might seem inconsequential when you hear it today, but tomorrow, in a different context, it could be revelatory."

TIME TO GET PERSONAL

"The people whose lives revolve around the thoroughbreds can be very set in their ways. The people whose focus is on the customer are constantly trying to introduce a better experience. Sometimes those two worlds clash."

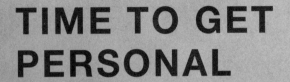

Bill Carstanjen
COO, Churchill Downs

Billy Johns
Unemployed Mover

How We Found the Boss

In the world of professional horse racing, one brand stands above all the rest. As the home of the Kentucky Derby, Churchill Downs is seen by fans and residents as a cultural institution rather than just a company. It so happens that the executive in charge of Churchill Downs also stands above all the rest; at six-foot-six, Bill Carstanjen is an imposing and highly recognizable figure, especially in an environment populated by diminutive jockeys. But Bill was so committed to his undercover mission of finding out what his employees truly think of his company that we had to find a way to make it work despite his lofty presence.

THE BOSS

Bill Carstanjen, COO.

HIS COVER

Billy Johns, whose moving company has gone out of business and who's the subject of a television documentary about entry-level jobs.

THE COMPANY

If there's any name that's synonymous with thoroughbred horse racing in the United States, it's Churchill Downs. Famed as the racetrack that hosts the Kentucky Derby, the oldest continually held sporting event in the United States, Churchill Downs was founded by Colonel M. Lewis Clark. Enamored by racecourses he'd visited on an 1873 European tour, Clark returned to Louisville, Kentucky, determined to open a world-class racetrack. Leasing 80 acres of land from his uncles, John and Henry Churchill, and selling membership subscriptions to raise construction funds, Clark had Churchill Downs up and running for its inaugural meet and the first running of the Kentucky Derby in 1875. Matt Winn and a group of local investors purchased the track in 1902, incorporated in 1928, and renamed the company Churchill Downs Incorporated (CDI) in 1942.

Publicly traded on the NASDAQ exchange, CDI now also owns Arlington Park racetrack in suburban Chicago, Calder Casino & Race Course in Miami, and Fair Grounds Race Course & Slots in New Orleans. Among CDI's other properties are off-track betting facilities in Illinois, Louisiana, and Kentucky; and television production, telecommunications, and racing services companies that support the corporation's core businesses of simulcasting and racing operations. CDI has a 50 percent interest in the HorseRacing TV network and has recently moved online with TwinSpires.com and Youbet.com, advance-deposit wagering services for all the company's racecourses, as well other thoroughbred and harness racing tracks across the globe. A company with historic roots in a tradition-bound industry, CDI is trying to maintain that rich culture while also leveraging its legacy to expand into faster-growing, technology-centered businesses.

HIS STORY

We're a nation obsessed with efficiency. If you're not multitasking, you're either a slacker or a Luddite. The management consultants have won, at least for now. If your work is not reducible to metrics then it doesn't count and if your numbers don't measure up or fall too fast, you're out the door. Spurred by advances in information technology, this quest to maximize performance has made Americans more productive workers. But in focusing on what things cost, we can forget the things that can't be measured. Sometimes we forget their real value.

Bill Carstanjen is in constant pursuit of knowledge. Bill's job as chief operating officer of Churchill Downs Incorporated (CDI) is to maximize profitability and analyze growth opportunities for a diversified $500 million company. At home he's a warm and caring husband and father of three, but at work the 42-year-old Bill is stoic and cerebral in manner, taking a detailed, analytical approach to problems. His glasses and restrained personality fit a man who spends much of his time studying spreadsheets and watching PowerPoint presentations. Bill's job places him firmly in one camp of a discernible cultural divide at CDI.

First there are the people at the "front end," who deal with the business demands and customers of all the varied operations under the CDI umbrella. These are a diverse group ranging from the executives who manage spreadsheets from offices (like Bill) to the managers and staff of the concession stands.

Then there are the people who don't have day-to-day contact with the customers. They are behind the scenes, in the backstretch, forming an agrarian village of trainers, jockeys, stable hands, and others whose lives revolve around the care of equine athletes. Some have a minimum of formal education. Many live in dormitories at the track. All are there because of their love for horses and horse racing.

Bill's career path, in contrast, has been dictated by opportunity rather than passion. The son and grandson of career naval officers, Bill spent most of his childhood moving from post to post, around the world. When it came time for college, he went to the University of California, Berkeley. Then, in defiance of family tradition, Bill went to Columbia University

PRODUCERS' NOTE
What You Didn't See

Along with gaining insight into a more connected management style and forging new connections with his employees, Bill accomplished something else during his undercover experience: he became more comfortable around horses. Bill spent part of his day working with Pete Love, a horse outrider, whose duties fall somewhere between those of a lifeguard and a paramedic. If a horse breaks loose without a rider, it's the outrider's job to chase after it and bring it in safely. His comfort level around horses made Pete the perfect candidate to reintroduce Bill to the majestic animals. Comparing horses to "big puppy dogs," Pete encouraged Bill to walk right up to the horse (called Junior) and give him some affection. Thanks to Pete's gentle guidance, Bill got back on a horse for the first time since his childhood years.

Law School, from which he graduated with honors. Bill went from law to the corporate world, joining General Electric, eventually rising to be managing director of a division brokering deals and acquisitions in the energy industry. Horses played no role in Bill's life before CDI. "To be honest, I find horses a little bit intimidating. I like to watch them . . . from afar."

He's had plenty of chance to observe them since joining CDI, but he's also spent much of his time helping diversify and reposition the company. Horse racing has had to face traumatic changes. When horse tracks were the only place where Americans could gamble legally, the industry could rely on making its money from those who walked through the gates. But as other opportunities for legal gambling sprung up, and technology made it possible to watch and bet on races from anywhere, the track lost its virtual monopoly. Today 90 percent of wagering on horse races happens somewhere other than at a track. To survive and continue to thrive, CDI has expanded beyond horse tracks, into

> *"The people whose lives revolve around the thoroughbreds can be very set in their ways because they've been doing things the same way for a long period of time. The people whose focus is on the customer are constantly trying to introduce new amenities, new entertainment options, and a different and better experience. Sometimes change isn't easy, and sometimes those two worlds clash."*

ventures like off-track betting parlors, casinos, television, and Internet gambling.

Bill fears that expansion and diversification threaten to exacerbate the organization's cultural divide. "The people whose lives revolve around the thoroughbreds can be very set in their ways because they've been doing things the same way for a long period of time. The people whose focus is on the customer are constantly trying to introduce new amenities, new entertainment options, and a different and better experience. Sometimes change isn't easy, and sometimes those two worlds clash."

The most efficient way, probably the only way, for Bill to get an unvarnished reading of how employees feel about all the changes being made in the company was to go undercover. "Since horse racing is a relatively small world, the minute I start

 PRODUCERS' NOTE
What You Didn't See

Although Gillian handles all the day-to-day responsibilities involved in taking care of the horses, her six-year-old son, Colin, is an official co-owner of Holding the Check, the horse that ran during Bill's undercover journey. While Gillian taught Bill all about the practical side of horse training, Colin gave Bill a lesson in getting the most out of one's employees. Apparently not content that Bill spent the previous day cleaning, feeding, and equipping his horse, Colin made some additional requests upon meeting Bill: Colin jokingly demanded that his horse's trainer-in-training fetch him some fried chicken, a bagel, and a "big cake." Apparently owning a horse is hungry work!

walking around either the backstretch or the frontside of one of our facilities, I'm noticed. I can see the cell phones getting pulled out to spread the word. That's true even when I go to tracks that aren't ours, because as a courtesy I always give my counterparts a call to let them know I'm coming. Since I came into the industry in a very senior role, I never had the experience of being able to go behind the scenes and walk around without being recognized and catered to. This was my chance." It didn't take long to see if his gamble would pay off.

JOB #1

Passion Isn't Always Enough
Stable Hand, Calder Race Course, Miami

Preparing for his first day undercover, Bill kept his fingers crossed that his minimal disguise of contact lenses, a few days' worth of stubble, and work clothes would be sufficient camouflage in a facility he visited often. He'd been coming to Calder often because it's one of the company's properties that has been going through the greatest changes. In an effort to attract more business and generate higher purses at the "meat and potatoes" track, CDI had invested $100 million in building a large casino alongside the racecourse.

Bill's job for the day was working with a trainer who didn't fit either of the stereotypical images of the profession. Neither a grizzled and gruff horseman nor a wealthy and aristocratic horsewoman, Gillian is instead a 30-year-old single mother who's struggling financially. Gillian spends her year bouncing between Calder and several other tracks, trying to earn enough

in prize-winning purses to pay for the care and feeding of herself and her son, as well as the eight horses under her care.

Gillian put Bill to work right away feeding her charges. She soon realized there was a problem. "When I climbed into a little stall with a 1,200 pound animal that really didn't like that I was in there, my blood pressure went up a little bit," Bill admitted. Seeing that the horses could sense his nervousness, Gillian looked for a task more in keeping with Bill's talents: helping scrub down the animals. Bill's aptitude with a hose and brush wasn't much better than his ability with the feed buckets. Although Bill managed to avoid getting kicked, he succeeded in hosing down his boss as well as the thoroughbred. Gillian diplomatically suggested that working with horses was perhaps not "Billy's" best choice for a future career.

Finally finding work for which Gillian thought he was qualified—cleaning out empty stables—Bill was relaxed enough to chat with Gillian about her business. What he learned wasn't encouraging. Gillian revealed that at the end of some months, she is often down to her last $200, out of which she has to feed her horses and her son, and pay for her car and her house. "Most of the people back here are struggling. If we didn't love it, we wouldn't be back here. I wouldn't suggest anyone get into this game."

Gillian explained that stalls at the track are allocated based on a trainer's success, but it's a Catch-22-like process. The more trainers win, the more stalls they get. But, to win more, they need more horses. And to have more horses, they need more stalls. One way for Gillian to start cracking this conundrum would be for her horse running later that day, Holding the Check, to win.

With the race set to begin, Gillian and Bill made their way to the stands. Gillian was praying and Bill was cheering as the horses left the gate. For a while it looked as though their invocations and exhortations were having an effect, as Holding the Check worked his way through the pack to take fourth place at the start of the homestretch. But it wasn't to be: he faded and finished out of the money. Gillian was upset. Her financial pressures hadn't got any easier.

"Our best asset is that the vast majority of our team members have a very deep personal commitment to this industry. It's more than a job to them. They're not here because it's the best-paying job, or it offers them the greatest financial opportunity for the future. They're here because they love what they do."

Bill recognized Gillian's very real financial predicament, and how precariously it was tied to her horses' performance. It was a problem facing all up-and-coming horse owners and trainers. "As the company that owns the tracks, we need people to want to get into this business," he explained. "At the end of the day, our future is going to depend on that. We can't just rely on the passion of a few folks who are born into the business." Diversification was one solution, but Gillian's ambivalence over the looming changes highlighted the challenges Bill faced in selling that answer. "The new casino could bring some of the big outfits and more money down to Calder," she accepted, "but I hope it won't result in little outfits like mine getting shoved out."

"Gillian provided a great lesson for me and for us as a company," Bill explained later. "We used to debate whether our greatest asset as a company was our brand, or the tradition of the Kentucky Derby. But I've learned our best asset is that the vast majority of our team members have a very deep personal commitment to this industry. It's more than a job to them. They're not here because it's the best-paying job nor because it offers them the greatest financial opportunity for the future. They're here because they love what they do."

JOB #2

Striking the Wrong Note

Bugler, Arlington Park, Arlington Heights IL

Often cited as the most beautiful racecourse in America, Arlington Park is rich in history and ambiance. Few things are more emblematic of that tradition than the Call to Post played by a formally dressed bugler. Never having played a musical instrument in his life, Bill didn't hold out much hope for succeeding as a bugler, but he thought it would be helpful to have personal experience of something so traditional.

Jean, the regular bugler, tried to help Bill overcome his inexperience by breaking out a couple of kazoos for them to practice on. Learning that Bill had never even played a kazoo, Jean patiently tried to get Bill to hum the Call to Post. Bill, trying his hardest, managed to sound like a day-old party balloon sputtering out its last stale bit of air.

Realizing that her task was hopeless, Jean sent Bill to put on his bugler's uniform, hoping the traditional togs would serve as a magical inspiration. Bill emerged, suffering from obvious stage fright and looking like a gigantic lawn orna-

"I thought that if I showed I was willing to go out there and make a complete fool of myself, that maybe the next time I pushed my kids or our team members to try something different, they'd have a more open mind."

ment. Sensing what was likely to come, Jean kept her final instructions simple. "Whatever you do, don't blow air into it. You have to buzz your lips. Just think buzz and air," she said, before sending Bill out for his performance. "I don't remember the last time I had a feeling like that in the pit of my stomach," Bill admitted. "My heart was pounding and I felt nauseous." Soon, so did his listeners.

The guest bugler was greeted by polite applause from the unsuspecting crowd. But the moment the first noise emerged, the crowd went silent. Sounding like a drunken duck who'd eaten an entire box of saltines, Bill produced a version of the Call to Post that set racing tradition back at least half a century.

Once it was over, Bill felt . . . relief. "To fail spectacularly was actually a liberating experience," he explained. Race fans the world over hope it was an experience he never feels the need to repeat. But it's not one he regrets. "I was thinking about my kids and about our team members at CDI, and all the times I ask them to do things outside their comfort zones. I thought that if I showed I was willing to go out there and make a complete fool of myself, that maybe the next time I pushed my kids or our team members to try something different, they'd have a more open mind."

JOB #3

The Long Way Home

Cleaner, Arlington Park, Arlington Heights IL

Bill's next undercover job was at the same facility, cleaning the luxury suites. Fear of being recognized as the COO had now been replaced by fear of being recognized as the morning's bugler. After meeting up with Denise, his coworker on the night shift, Bill realized he needn't worry about anyone noticing him: the facility was deserted.

Denise, a single mother of four, had been working at Arlington Park for only seven months. She had begun working in the general seating area, but when management noticed how hard she worked, they promoted her to clean the two floors of luxury suites. Denise showed the pride and dedication that had gotten her promoted when explaining the importance of the job to Bill. "Suite level has to be very well kept, very clean," she instructed. "Nothing is to be left on floors, on tables, or on bar areas. We clean and dust everything, and vacuum. When you finish you want to look back at the room and admire it like it's a fine work of art."

Bill's work was more like a finger painting. He was neither fastidious nor quick enough. "Billy wouldn't be good at this job," Denise confided. "He's just not cleaning material, and he's slowing me down tremendously." Speed was important to Denise because she commuted 90 minutes each way to work. Her promotion hadn't come with a raise, and she couldn't afford a home any closer to Arlington Park.

When they'd finished at around midnight, Denise confessed she was sometimes frightened at having to walk the considerable distance from the grandstand to her car through the dark and forbidding parking lot. Escorting staff wasn't part of the ever present security detail's responsibilities, so Bill walked Denise to her car.

Watching Denise head off on her drive home, Bill reflected on the irony of the day. "I've been in all these suites on race days, when each is packed with a party, and I've never thought of all the work that goes into cleaning them up quickly for the next day. Denise isn't a horse person, but she's every bit as dedicated and hard working as the people on the backstretch. She deserves just as much respect, and she's as important to the track as they are."

JOB #4

A Youthful View Across the Divide

Groom/Press Box Coordinator, Arlington Park, Arlington Heights IL

Bill wanted to learn about what the younger people in the industry felt and thought, so for his fourth job undercover he worked with Roxanne, a 24-year-old who, unusually, worked on both the backstretch and frontside of the track.

Petite with long red hair and freckles, Roxanne grew up in Hot Springs, Arkansas, and had made the move to Illinois on her own to pursue her goal of a career in horse racing. From 4 A.M. until 8 A.M., Roxanne worked as a groom on the backstretch. Then she quickly cleaned up and moved to the frontside, where she served as press box coordinator.

Bill caught up with Roxanne on her return from escorting the thoroughbreds to and from their morning workouts, mounted on Shorty. The placid pony's job was to keep the sometimes skittish thoroughbreds calm. Helping Roxanne remove Shorty's tack and give him a bath was much less nerve wracking for Bill than dealing with the high-strung and much larger thoroughbreds. Impressed by her initiative, Bill asked Roxanne what her ultimate career goal was. "Becoming president of Churchill Downs," Roxanne said offhandedly.

Meeting back up with a now more formally dressed Roxanne in the press box, Bill asked her about working on both sides of the company's perceived cultural divide. Roxanne explained that it was part of her plan to move up in the industry. "Not all the frontside people understand the people on the backstretch. I think it helps to have people who are versatile enough that they can go back and forth." Roxanne also pointed out that "Billy" wasn't dressed appropriately for the press box, so he needed to leave before the media began to arrive.

Later, Bill reflected that Roxanne's idea wasn't just an expression of youthful idealism; it was a pragmatic response to real need. "In my times previously visiting the backstretch, there was always a level of formality that led me to believe the people were insular," Bill explained. "But being undercover I saw that formality disappear. There was no tension, and the people were very quick to accept me. That's one reason it's really important to have people like Roxanne, who can bridge the two sides of the business, working for us."

JOB #5

It Was Right in Front of Him

Jockey's Valet, Arlington Park, Arlington Heights IL

For his final undercover assignment, Bill worked as a jockey's valet. These are unsung heroes of horse racing whose job it is to get the jockeys ready for their rides throughout the course of a day's races.

Outside the jockey's room, Bill met Kenny, a wiry ex-jockey nearly two feet shorter than the undercover executive. Kenny hurried Bill over to the Ladies Jockey's Room to introduce him to Inez, who'd be their jockey for the day. Kenny sped through hallways and in and out of back rooms, all the time wielding an omnipresent overloaded clipboard that held all the information about his jockey's races for the day. With the track-side announcer constantly intoning how many minutes were left between races, Kenny's pace was relentless. He led Bill on what seemed like a high-speed scavenger hunt through a warren of tunnels.

Speeding down the hall back into the jockey's room, the former jockey and the lanky undercover executive made for a scene out of a Mutt and Jeff comic, the former's short quick steps keeping him well ahead of the latter, with his long loping strides. Whenever Bill seemed lost, Kenny directed him back to the clipboard, hammering home that "it's your life source for the day." At one point they misplaced each other, Bill running down one hallway to look for Kenny, and Kenny running down another to look for Bill.

It turned out to be a good day for Kenny because Inez won three races, meaning three paychecks for the valet. The valets receive 10 percent of the jockey's winnings. Sitting down to review Bill's performance for the day after the pressure was over, Kenny praised him for his hard work. The generous valet then

slipped the undercover executive $200 for his help during the day. Kenny encouraged Bill, saying that all the rookie needed to be a good valet was more experience, explaining that he himself had the advantage of growing up at the track. "My little girl grew up here too. I was going to teach her to be a rider." Pointing out to Bill the formal picture of a young woman that was on top of his clipboard all day, Kenny explained that his daughter had passed away in March, at the age of 20, from a congenital heart defect. "She was going to be my jockey, my Meghan. She used to come out and watch Inez every day." Kenny's hardboiled exterior showed some cracks when he spoke of his late daughter. "Well, now she's an angel in heaven. She's in a better place, and I know I'll see her again one day."

Bill was speechless, overwhelmed almost as much by his shame as his sorrow. Up until that moment he hadn't looked closely enough at the picture to see it was a memorial card, and he'd never asked Kenny about the picture during the course of the day. "When I first glanced at it I could tell it was his daughter," Bill recalled, "but I focused on the data on the clipboard that related to the races." Choking up, Bill ashamedly admitted, "I should have noticed earlier, and I should have asked him about it."

Even after his experience was over, Bill couldn't let go of his failure to see the obvious. "It would have taken me maybe two seconds to read the words under the picture, two seconds to be observant about something personal. But I divided the world into personal and work, and to be as efficient as I could, I focused only on the work piece." It turned out to be one of the most important lessons Bill took away from his undercover experience.

HE REVEALS THE TRUTH

Rested, recovered, and back in his familiar corporate uniform, Bill called his executive team to a meeting back in Arlington Park to discuss his experience. Telling his lieutenants how enlightening the undercover experience was, Bill explained that they all had an obligation to be better managers.

"Two of the most important things I took away from this experience are the realization that the split in our culture isn't as profound as we'd feared, and we really don't have a problem with resistance to change," Bill revealed. What he and others had perceived as insularity among those on the backstretch was actually reticence and the fear of not seeing how their way of life fit into the company's future. "Everyone I spoke with and everywhere I went on the backstretch, there was a real commitment to wanting the company to succeed and a willingness to accept the changes that might involve. I think the problem has been one of communication and leadership," Bill confessed. "When you dictate to people and don't tell them how they can help, they think you don't need them. Our people just want to understand the changes better and most of all, understand what their part will be and how they can help."

Asked how he planned on changing his own management approach, Bill was candid. "Here's the problem with my job," he explained. "A lot of the way I access information and work with employees is very impersonal; it's through spreadsheets and presentations. That's the best way for me to be efficient with my time and do as much as I can for the company in the course of the day. But I need to give up some of that drive to maximize efficiency. To really be the best team member I can be, I've got to set aside the time to make things a little bit more personal. Even though that means giving up some efficiency and control over my time, it's worth it."

"I think the problem has been one of communication and leadership," Bill confessed. "When you dictate to people and don't tell them how they can help, they think you don't need them. Our people just want to understand the changes better and most of all, understand what their part will be and how they can help."

Having briefed his managers, Bill could meet with his coworkers from the prior week, all of whom had been brought to Chicago for reasons unknown. All were curious and more than a bit apprehensive, though Kenny was thrilled by his first ride in a limo.

Gillian was happy to see her less than stellar stable hand again. After revealing his true identity, Bill told Gillian how much he admired her grit and determination in pursuing a career that she loved, even though it could be very difficult financially. He realized she needed three or four more stalls, and Bill promised that she'd get them after the casino opened. He added that if she wanted to come work for the company full-time, he had a job for her. Overjoyed, Gillian said, "I don't know whether to laugh or cry."

Denise was surprised but glad to see her cleaning partner, and was stunned when he revealed his real role in the company. "Your passion really came through," Bill explained, thanking her for giving him a chance to get to know her and learn how the night shift worked. "With respect to your feeling unsafe at night, we're going to have a new policy that says you'll get an escort to your car any time you or any of our other employees at night wants. I also know your commute is very long. We have off-track betting parlors that are closer to your home, so if you're interested, we will offer you a position in one of those facilities." Denise tearfully explained that it felt good that some-one recognized all the hard work she did.

Roxanne laughed in recognition when "Billy" entered the office, and said that she liked his suit, even before he told her who he really was. Bill explained that he admired Roxanne's ini-tiative and willingness to just roll up her sleeves and start work-ing different jobs. He said he was going to give her a chance to do that once more by offering her a job in the marketing department at Churchill Downs in Louisville. "I've warned the racetrack president that you're coming and that he should look out for his job," he joked. Roxanne, beaming, responded that she felt "excited, scared, but super stoked. I can't wait to get to Louisville and learn something new."

Kenny was immediately relieved when he saw "Billy" enter the office. "How's my valet?" he asked. Bill confessed that he didn't think he could ever do Kenny's job and that the valet's passion for what he does really came through. "I thought one thing we could do at Arlington Park that you might appreciate and might have meant something to Meghan would be to name a race after her on opening day next year." As his eyes began to water, Kenny reiterated that his late daughter was "his heart and soul." Bill explained that they'd like Kenny, Inez, other valets, and family and friends to come to

"Folks in this business gave me a chance, showed me their world, and didn't hold my not being from their world against me. They taught me an important lesson: the most important things in life start with human interaction. They start with talking and caring. That's something we all need to understand better. I think it's something I lost sight of a little bit, but I'm absolutely going to be better at my job because of this experience."

the winner's circle after the race to present the winner's trophy. "That would be special," Kenny said, choking up. "She'll see that." Getting his emotions back under control, he told Bill to come see him any time he wanted to be a valet for a day.

Putting that offer aside for the moment, Bill went outside to speak to the headquarters and track staff who'd gathered around the Arlington Park paddock. The man who had come to his position atop one of the most iconic companies by happenstance rather than passion had a chance to show his newfound love for this industry and its people. After showing video evidence of his being a horse of a different color, Bill offered something of a confession to his employees: "I'm a real fish out of water. I'm not from the backstretch, and I didn't grow up around horses. But the folks in this business gave me a chance, showed me their world, and didn't hold my not being from their world against me. They taught me an important lesson: the most important things in life start with human interaction. They start with talking and caring. That's something we all need to understand better. I think it's something I lost sight of a little bit, but I'm absolutely going to be better at my job because of this experience."

As the excitement subsided, Bill had a moment to reflect privately on going undercover. "I was a straight man in a television show, but while there was a TV show going on all around me, I tried to focus on getting to understand the company's culture better and getting to know our people better. I really think that what was important to my team members wasn't that I went undercover, but that someone in upper management was willing to spend time and give an honest effort to learn what they do and what their lives are like."

SINCE THE SHOW

★ **Denise** has started a new job at Arlington Park that came with a raise.

★ **Roxanne** worked in the marketing department of Churchill Downs racetrack during the buildup to the Kentucky Derby. She's now working at the press box at Churchill Downs. She's thrilled with the opportunities she's received, but she misses Shorty.

★ **Gillian** has received the additional stalls Bill promised, and is expanding her training business. Her pride and joy, a docile colt named Starship Voyage, has become a regular winner at the newly renovated Calder Casino & Race Course.

★ April 29, 2010, opening day at Arlington Park, saw the inaugural running of the Meghan Samantha Rice Memorial Race, honoring Kenny's late daughter. The entire Arlington Park jockey colony and all the valets joined Kenny and his family in the winner's circle. So did Bill, who announced that Meghan's race would now be a regular part of Arlington Park's opening-day race card.

★ **Bill** is still COO of Churchill Downs Incorporated. He's found a way of giving other managers in the business an experience similar to his undercover one. It's a program called Walk a Mile in Someone Else's Shoes. "We're taking managers and for a day putting them into frontline jobs, either interacting with customers, taking care of the facilities, or working on the backstretch. The idea is for the managers to get a chance to learn about the lives and jobs of frontline employees. It also means those employees see that management appreciates the challenges they face and recognizes how hard they work."

The undercover experience has had a lasting impact on how Bill operates as an executive. He's making a conscious effort not to make assumptions about people based on their appearance or job. "I walked by a number of people at Calder and Arlington Park who I'd worked with regularly in the past in my role as COO. But they looked right through me. My level of disguise was far below even the Inspector Clouseau level. I'm six-foot-six, so I automatically stand out. But I was wearing work clothes rather than a suit and tie, so those people just looked right through me. I understand we all live in a complicated world that bombards us with information and stimuli all the time, so it's natural to mentally pigeonhole people based on the message their appearance sends. But from now on I'm going to fight this tendency, and tell all my managers to do their best not to define employees by their own limited expectations of them."

The efficiency-driven executive is also relaxing his tendency to maximize every moment of his working life. "I'm giving people more time than ever before, just leaving five hours blank on my calendar, for example, to walk a facility and observe and talk to people. Spreadsheets are still a great way to learn lots of information quickly. But I've learned that the best information comes from talking with people. That's not something you can budget five minutes for in an effort to maximize efficiency. You need to put away the papers, close the briefcase, turn off the BlackBerry, look people in the eye, and talk with them for as long as it takes."

LOOKING FOR FULFILLMENT

"The competition is moving very quickly; there's no time to rest. There's no question that I'm a fast-paced individual. It's just the way I'm wired."

Michael Rubin
CEO, GSI Commerce

Gary Rogers
Seasonal Worker

> ### How We Found the Boss
>
> Usually by the time someone reaches the position of CEO in corporate America, they've been around a long time. But there are exceptions and one remarkable one is Michael Rubin, Founder and CEO of GSI Commerce. We wanted a young, energetic chief executive to contrast with the seasoned corporate veterans who ran most of the companies we were to feature. Having grown the company he founded to more than $1 billion in revenue by age 38, Michael fit the bill perfectly.

THE BOSS

Michael Rubin, founder and CEO.

HIS COVER

Gary Rogers, an unemployed sporting goods salesman taking part in a television documentary about seasonal jobs.

HIS COMPANY

GSI Commerce may not be a household name, but it's the on-line engine behind many more recognizable brands. A worldwide leader in e-commerce, multichannel retailing, and interactive marketing, the King of Prussia, Pennsylvania–based firm runs the online operations of some of America's most successful companies. Among its more than 500 clients are the NFL, Toys"R"Us, Timberland, PBS, Calvin Klein, Major League Baseball, Aeropostale, GNC, RadioShack, NASCAR, Burberry, the NBA, Levis, Ralph Lauren, Bath & Body Works, Dick's Sporting Goods, and Ace Hardware. The company provides full service e-commerce solutions for its customers, from Web site design and interactive marketing to product fulfillment and customer service. In 2009, the firm had net revenues of $1 billion. Its more than 5,000 regular employees work in a Philadelphia-area headquarters, five customer care facilities that handle approximately 18 million contacts, and seven fulfillment centers totaling 2.7 million square feet, which manage more than 21 million orders a year.

HIS STORY

There are two kinds of entrepreneurs. First are those for whom business is a means to an end. They're on a mission, focused on bringing to market a singular product or service that they've developed, and to which they're willing to dedicate their lives. Then there are those for whom business is an end in itself. They're not on a mission because they've no finite goal in mind, other than winning. For them, business isn't a way of life; it *is* their life.

Michael Rubin, founder of GSI Commerce, could be the poster boy for this latter group. One thing that sets Michael apart from all the others who live to work is that he's been that way since seventh grade. Although at 38, some may classify Michael as mature among Internet CEOs, few started their careers earlier than he did. At 13 he started a ski-tuning business in the basement of his parents' suburban Philadelphia

PRODUCERS' NOTE
What You Didn't See

There are many stories of Michael's early precociousness. One of our favorites: when Michael earned his driver's license at age 16, he didn't have to beg his parents to buy him a car. With several successful business ventures already under his belt, lack of capital was not a problem for this young entrepreneur. However, his parents still held some degree of authority over Michael and—concerned with their son's safety—made him promise to buy a sensible vehicle as his first car. Michael happily complied with his parents' wishes and bought himself a clunky station wagon. He parked it in his parents' driveway and took it out every morning to go to school or work. Michael got his car, his parents got their peace of mind, and everyone was appeased. However, it's a good thing that Michael's parents didn't check the mileage on that station wagon. If they had, they would have found that Michael would drive it only approximately five blocks every day—to where he parked his other car that his parents didn't know about: a Porsche. He would then switch cars, leave his station wagon in the dust, and drive to school in style.

home. Using the profits and connections from the ski tuning business, Michael opened a ski and sporting goods store when just a sophomore in high school. Too young to sign a lease on his own, he lobbied his mother, a psychiatrist, to co-sign. When she turned him down, he refused to take "no" for an answer. In classic teenage fashion, he turned to his other parent. Michael's pitch to his veterinarian dad was more successful (in part because he conveniently omitted the fact that his mom had already turned him down). His dad's only stipulation was that Michael pursue his college education. It turned out to be a short-lived pursuit.

When he arrived for his freshman year at Villanova University, Michael already had a chain of four retail stores in Pennsylvania and New York. It took only a few weeks for Michael, his parents, and Villanova to realize that college wasn't for him. Leaving school, he dedicated himself full-time to business. He started a discount sporting goods distribution company, and soon after acquired a major stake in a footwear business. Because that firm was listed on the NASDAQ Exchange, 23-year-old Michael became CEO of a publicly traded company. Combining his businesses in 1997, Michael formed Global Sports, Inc. But before the ink on the incorporating documents was even dry, his ever alert antenna picked up on a new industry that he suspected had incredible potential: e-commerce. Many of his retail customers had grumbled to him about the new competition they faced in the on-line marketplace and had shared their trepidation about building and operating a Web site. Michael knew an opportunity when he saw it.

Briefly testing the water with an e-commerce division, Michael made a dramatic dive into the Internet business. Believing that it would be established brands, not Internet start-ups, that would one day dominate e-commerce, Michael divested his company of all its legacy operations and committed completely to the new business. The firm expanded beyond its initial sporting goods focus, and by 2002 when it was formally renamed GSI Commerce, it had become one of the world's leaders in e-commerce.

Possessed with boundless energy, Michael is a high-speed perpetual motion machine. Seventy-hour workweeks are his norm. He is admittedly addicted to his BlackBerry, and sometimes wakes in the middle of the night to check e-mails and calls from Asia and Europe. Michael even talks at a rapid clip. "People sometimes think I'm speaking a different language," he admitted. Michael is often compared to the Energizer Bunny (who keeps going, and going, and going). Luckily, he's married to an understanding woman who accepts that this is who he is. "I was the CEO of a $150 million public company when I met my wife 11 years ago (at age 26); so the lifestyle I lead now is no different."

> *"I get out of the bubble as much as anyone—talking to people in the halls and in the cafeteria—but it's easy to become isolated in the corner office."*

Michael made a conscious effort to slow down his speech because so many people were having problems understanding him. And, at his wife's insistence, he's trying not to keep his BlackBerry on the bedside table at night, putting it in the drawer instead. But at peak season he can't help but peek. Having a child has also changed him—up to a point. "My four-year-old daughter definitely has expectations of me. She's very authoritative. I feel like I work for her when I come home." But his other child, GSI, is also demanding. "We're in a fast-paced industry and we're a fast-growing company. Competition is moving very quickly; there's no time to rest. There's no question that I'm a fast-paced individual. It's just the way I'm wired."

There hasn't been much time during these past few years of meteoric growth for Michael to maintain a hands-on feel for operations. "I get out of the bubble as much as anyone—talking to people in the halls and in the cafeteria—but it's easy to become isolated in the corner office. My day is generally a series of nonstop meetings, mostly with external parties." Michael saw going undercover as a way to compensate for this unavoidable isolation and outside focus. "It would give me a chance to do the jobs that are so important to the company. It would also be a chance for me to figure out how the morale was in the different areas of the company. "

Ever in search of a challenge, Michael decided to go undercover at the peak time for his business. "We make 70 percent of our profits during the holiday shopping season, so everything is about nailing that peak time. I decided to go undercover at the most stressful time of year, when everything is going crazy, because I'll be able to see how my team is playing during the most important moment of the game." The company's typical staff of 5,000 doubles during the last quarter of the calendar year, with seasonal workers brought in to help meet the productivity demands. This provided Michael with a ready alias as one of those seasonal workers—handling phone calls, picking products, packing boxes, and loading trucks for a week during peak season.

The man who lived to work looked forward to spending time with those who work for a living. Michael fully expected to learn a great deal and come back with ideas for changes that needed to be made. He didn't anticipate that they'd be life lessons and that the necessary changes would be personal.

JOB #1

Neither High nor Tight

GSI Fulfillment Center, Richwood KY

GSI's Richwood fulfillment center is the fourth-largest automated sorting facility in the United States. Covering 543,000 square feet, it has the capacity to ship more than 110,000 orders per day. Michael's job on his first day undercover would be helping get those boxes out the door.

Matt, the floor supervisor, greeted "Gary" then quickly ushered him to where he'd be working, loading trucks with Rashelle. Also a seasonal worker, Rashelle had been on the job for only a couple of weeks. A 37-year-old divorced mother of two, Rashelle was tending bar when she drove by the fulfillment center and saw the sign advertising for seasonal help. Unhappy with the hours and environment at her bartender job, she jumped at the opportunity.

Rashelle immediately took Michael under her wing, showing him the best way to pack the delivery truck, as if she'd been doing the job for years rather than days. Energetic and enthusiastic, she explained that the key was to put boxes of the same size on top of each other and to pack the truck "high and tight." A conveyer system, projecting into the truck's interior, immediately began marching boxes into the truck at a steady rate. Michael and Rashelle had two hours to fill the back of an 18-wheel truck with cardboard cartons.

Working side by side, they began stacking boxes, trying to keep up with the steady supply that kept advancing down the ramp. Rashelle's side of the truck was soon filled with orderly, tightly arranged columns of cardboard; Michael's side looked like the mass of empty gift boxes a child would hastily shove under a Christmas tree. While Michael griped about the pace (and for the first time in his life, secretly wished for orders to slow down), Rashelle laughed and admitted that the job was a good workout. Making small talk while they worked, Michael learned that Rashelle was hoping to get a permanent job offer from the company so that she could help pay for her sons' college tuitions.

"I went in there with a lot confidence. I figured, I'm a young guy, I started the business, I can do any job within the company. Well, I got my butt whipped."

Despite Michael's secret wishes, the boxes traveling down the ramp didn't slow down. As the two loaders progressively backed their way out the trailer, Michael's disorderly piles began tumbling. More concerned with doing damage control on his teetering stacks than with being able to grab the onslaught of new boxes continuing to come down the ramp, Michael was soon tossing boxes back to the top of the pile, much like bailing out a boat taking on water. At one point, as his efforts became more frantic, Michael's attempt at a backhand box flip caught Rashelle square in the face.

"I felt horrible," Michael recalled. "We were only halfway out of the truck and I was already exhausted and dripping with sweat. I was worried I'd hurt her and that she'd be really upset. But she was such a great sport—she shrugged it off, asked me to be more careful, and just kept going." Clearly, the Energizer Bunny had met his match.

As her side of the trailer neatly filled up, Rashelle, bravely risking further assault, shifted over to Michael's side to help him stem the tide of falling boxes. With their allotted time just about over, Matt came back to check on their work. Less than pleased with the job Michael had done, Matt explained that the shipping company wasn't going to be happy if its driver opened the door and boxes fell out, nor would customers be pleased to receive damaged products. Diplomatically suggesting that loading trucks wasn't "Gary's" strength, Matt shifted Michael and Rashelle over to the sorting station.

Michael did better at the less physically demanding, slower-paced job of sorting boxes by region before placing them on palettes. Rashelle demonstrated an innovation of her own that boosted productivity by 25 percent: placing destination bar code stickers on her arm so that she could enter info into the tracking system more quickly.

The day was both exhausting and enlightening for Michael. "I went in there with a lot confidence. I figured, I'm a young guy, I started the business, I can do any job within the company. Well, I got my butt whipped. I had to admit that I'm not cut out to do the kind of physical jobs that are crucial to the success of GSI. My personal trainer needs to be fired because he has never

given me a workout comparable to the one I got that day loading boxes. We've invested over $30 million in automating this
facility; but I've learned that when it comes to loading trucks,
it's all about physical labor, and that it's an incredibly tough
job." Compensation for his fatigue was seeing how Rashelle,
a seasonal employee, not only worked hard but came up with
ideas to be more productive. As physically taxing as Michael
found his first day undercover, his second day would cause him
even more pain. But this time, it would be emotional.

JOB #2

From Heartbreak to Anger
GSI Call Center, Melbourne FL

Despite having to fly from Kentucky down to Florida for his
next job, Michael was excited. He'd be working in one of the
company's call centers as an escalations operator, handling customers with issues that customer service was unable to resolve.
"Escalations is probably the most stressful job in the entire
company. Every phone call is from someone with a big problem, and your goal is to solve it and turn someone who's angry
into a customer for life. I thought it would be the single best
source of information for me as CEO, because it would let me
see everything that didn't work well." He got his wish.

Michael's trainer for the day was Adam, a 25-year-old with
the warmth and wholesomeness of a young Ron Howard. The
even-tempered escalations manager was almost literally born for
his job: his parents owned a call center, and he had been in and
around them his entire life. Preparing Michael to be screamed at,

Adam stressed the importance of using a calm voice, explaining that the main thing to do is apologize and then try to end with the caller being satisfied. Listening to Adam field call after call dealing with problems, Michael was struck by how smoothly he handled every problem, no matter how frustrated or angry the caller was initially. "Adam could be a hostage negotiator," Michael quipped admiringly.

When it came time to take calls himself, Michael found apologizing easy, but he struggled to find remedies for difficulties or ways to appease the customers. With coaching, Michael was eventually able to placate his callers, but he found it draining. Saying that he didn't think he had the personality for the job, Michael asked Adam how he did it. Adam explained that the key for him was perspective: "This is how I look at it: if their order is their biggest problem, I'm going to do everything I can to get their issue resolved so they'll be satisfied and calm by the end of the call."

On their break, Adam described how much he appreciated GSI, saying that he'd come to the company a little more than a year before, after being fired by a cell phone company. "It was a very bad personal situation," he revealed. "My only child died. I wasn't able to go into work that day, so they said my services were no longer needed." Stunned, Michael listened as Adam related how his infant daughter's heart failed at birth, and how he and his fiancée had put their wedding plans on hold in order to save money to buy the burial plots adjoining their daughter's grave.

At a loss for words other than to offer his condolences, Michael shook his head in disbelief at the unfathomable price Adam had paid for the gift of perspective. "Sometimes it's nice to be able to hide behind your desk, do your job, and not get close to these things," Michael admitted later. "To hear what he went through broke my heart, and it really made me miss my family. I was definitely not prepared for anything like that."

Later the same day, Michael shadowed a different escalations operator so that he could better learn the system. A confident woman with short-cropped hair and tattooed arms, 30-year-old Danielle was normally a sales agent, but she had been brought over to escalations to help handle the peak-season rush.

It took only a few minutes for Michael to see that Danielle's approach differed from Adam's. Although her tone was calm and solicitous, Danielle could also be confrontational rather than empathic. Trying to handle a difficult call with a customer whose order hadn't been filled properly (through no fault of her own), Michael struggled to find a way to mollify the caller's anger. Danielle coached Michael to be assertive and take control of the situation. "You have to put her in her place. I know your goal is to please her, but you have to understand that sometimes we can't. It's impossible," she stressed. With Michael making no progress, Danielle took over the call herself.

Whereas Adam would have let the caller vent her frustration before he apologized, Danielle went toe to toe with the customer. The caller suggested that Danielle didn't understand the problem. Danielle disagreed, saying she *did* understand the problem. The caller went into a description of the problem with her order. Danielle interrupted, saying that the caller wasn't giving her a chance to speak. The customer became further exasperated. Danielle suggested that she take the matter up with the corporate offices. The caller hung up.

Barely able to contain his anger at seeing a customer treated this way, Michael asked to take a break. "I went from heartbroken to extreme frustration and anger in a matter of minutes," he revealed. "That's not the kind of attitude that I expect from my employees. I think Danielle had a chip on her shoulder, and she wanted to prove she was right rather than focusing on the customer's needs. That is not acceptable in my company. She's lucky that the show was being filmed and I didn't want to blow my cover in front of the employees. Otherwise, she'd have been walked out of there right then."

What Michael *did* do was break his cover with the supervisor of the call center, outside the sight of the rest of the staff and the cameras. Michael asked for and received the name and telephone number of the caller who'd hung up, and then called her back. It took a lot of explaining to convince her that he really was the CEO of the company—undercover. "She thought I was crazy," Michael laughed. Apologizing for the problems with her order, Michael told her she'd receive the product at no charge.

Although Michael was still fuming, he tried to view the situation as an opportunity. "We'll process more than 20 million orders this year and handle over 15 million contacts, so I know not every transaction is going to go perfectly. One satisfied customer tells five other people, but an unhappy customer tells 50. Adam was great for word of mouth. Danielle was bad. A problem like this was the last thing I wanted to find undercover, but I'm glad I found it. The first thing I decided was that we need to be more discerning about who we allow to handle escalations. The second decision was that we have to intensify our training of that handpicked group."

JOB #3

Not Quick Enough

GSI Fulfillment Center, Richwood KY

Michael headed back to Richwood, hoping that the day would be less of an emotional roller coaster. He'd be working as a single-item packer, evaluated on how many boxes he could pack and label in as short a period of time as possible. The faster he worked, the more profit he'd make for his company, and with peak season producing six times the usual numbers of orders to be filled, Michael had a golden opportunity to personally contribute to his company's bottom line.

Greg, the packing supervisor, brought Michael over to observe and work alongside Shannon, one of the facility's most skilled packers. Married, with two teenage sons, Shannon had given up her job at a bank to work at GSI. She certainly wasn't keeping banker's hours anymore: once the holiday rush began, she found herself working seven days a week.

First, Shannon brought Michael over to watch her pack items. As she taped the boxes, packed items, sealed the boxes, and added the right labels (all with the deceptively quick speed and precision of a teller counting out a stack of dollar bills), Shannon drove home that the goal was to pack 90 items an hour, or one every 40 seconds. Without a trace of boasting, Shannon stated that she actually packed 110 to 150 boxes an hour herself. Michael, agape at Shannon's proficiency, was intimidated, but still willing to rise to the challenge. Although nervous about trying to match her speed, he was sure he'd get a handle on the procedure quickly.

Once again, Michael's self-confidence was misplaced. He handled the cartons, tape gun, and labels with the ineptitude of a parent assembling a miniature Hogwarts on Christmas morning. After 90 minutes, Greg informed Michael that he was averaging only 40 boxes packed per hour. He needed to show some improvement if he wanted to keep his job.

Over lunch, Shannon offered encouragement to the now apprehensive Michael. Commiserating with him, she described how the seven-day-a-week schedule was hard on her family. Normally much of her free time went to volunteer efforts that

supported her boys' football teams, but GSI's busy holiday schedule was making it hard to keep up.

Back at their packing stations after lunch, Michael had renewed resolve to meet his targets. Unfortunately, resolve and Shannon's coaching weren't enough. Rushing to pick up the pace, he tore one shipping label and misapplied another. By 3 P.M. Greg was back, bearing the evidence of Michael's shortcomings. Holding the box with the torn label and the other with the misapplied label, he informed Michael that the labeling issues, combined with the less than satisfactory numbers, meant that GSI no longer needed his services. Admitting to himself that he was more nervous packing boxes than he ever was in his role as CEO, an embarrassed Michael had been fired, for the first time

PRODUCERS' NOTE
What You Didn't See

In addition to her lightning-quick packing skills and her devotion to her sons' football teams, Shannon contributes to her community through working at a bingo hall a couple of nights a week. The night after Michael was "fired" for failing to pack enough boxes in the allotted time, he accompanied Shannon to her bingo game. Believe it or not, this was the first time Michael had ever played bingo—I guess starting your own company at age 13 doesn't leave too much spare time for casual games of chance. Michael ended up thoroughly enjoying his first foray into the world of bingo—he ended up as the caller for several games himself. Thanks to Shannon, 38-year-old Michael was able to experience some of the typical pleasures he never got to enjoy as a child.

in his life, and from his own company. He realized that the fault was entirely his own. "I thought they did a great job overall in giving me direction and encouragement. I just couldn't get the job done. Shannon's job is much more difficult than mine."

Seeing someone so skilled at her job and dedicated to the company was inspiring for Michael. But it also led him to reevaluate the way he'd looked at the relationship between people and machinery. "When I decided to go undercover, I'd assumed I'd find people who were trying to keep up with the technology and machines that we had. But Shannon packed boxes faster than the packing slips came out; she's quicker than the computer, and she's not the only one. That's a testament to how incredibly good our people are at their jobs and how they, not our technology, are the reason for our success."

JOB #4

Race to the Finish
GSI Fulfillment Center, Louisville KY

Knowing he'd screwed up loading trucks, handling problem calls, and packing boxes, the ever competitive Michael was resolved to go down swinging. This time, however, he'd lowered his expectations a bit. No longer looking to demonstrate his mastery, Michael said that his goal for his last undercover job was simply not to bring the Louisville fulfillment center operation to its knees.

Michael would be working the night shift as a picker. When orders are placed at a client's Web site, they are transmitted to a fulfillment center. If the order contains multiple items, it's assigned to a picker, who collects the items together from their various locations in the massive warehouse so that they can be shipped in one box.

Arriving at 7 P.M. for his shift, Michael was met by Cameron, his trainer for the day. A compact, solidly built man, Cameron had Michael tag along as he sped up and down the aisles at a brisk pace, gathering products. Wielding his hand-mounted computer–bar code reader and pulling a cart through the cavernous facility, Cameron was like an adventurer in a video game searching out treasures and rewards. He knew the layout of the warehouse like the back of his electronically augmented hand. Cameron planned his movements for maximum efficiency, hustling down one aisle to grab an ordered item and back to the

PRODUCERS' NOTE
What You Didn't See

When Cameron was living on the streets of Detroit as a teenager, a kindhearted family took him in and offered him a place to stay. The patriarch of the family—a man Cameron refers to as his "godfather"—took an active role in Cameron's life, helping him pursue school and encouraging him to play basketball. Cameron credits this man with literally saving his life.

After Cameron returned to Kentucky, he lost touch with his godfather . . . until *Undercover Boss.* For the finale of the episode, we were able to track down Cameron's godfather, who was happy to make the trip down for the occasion. To say that the reunion was emotional would be an understatement—and it was an absolute thrill for Cameron to introduce his daughter to the man who made such a momentous difference in his life.

cart, then up another aisle where he could grab a second item. Motivated by Cameron's competitive urge to excel, Michael was quickly drawn into the challenge of the hunt.

Agreeing that the introductory training session had been a success, the two pickers took a break so that Cameron could share a quick visit with his young daughter. As he and his daughter played at the pool table in the break room, Cameron told Michael that because he worked such long hours and night shifts, he didn't get to see his daughter as much as he'd like. For Cameron that was especially painful because of his own background. As a teen, Cameron lived on the streets of Detroit for a time before returning to Kentucky. A single parent after the death of his wife in an auto accident, Cameron was determined to be the kind of parent that he never had.

"I'm a good husband, but I could be a better husband. I'm a good father, but I could be a great father. The most valuable lesson I got from spending time undercover was about how I could be a better person."

Back on the floor, Cameron playfully challenged Michael to a contest to see who could pick the most products during the rest of their shift. Michael, knowing his was a lost cause, took the bait anyway. As the two men raced up and down the aisles, Cameron personified economy of motion, whereas Michael was like a crazed cartoon character spinning his legs trying to gain traction. As they passed each other in the aisles and checked on each other's progress, Cameron's teasing trash talk was spiced with encouragement and insistence that Michael not let his competitive drive lead him to make mistakes. Cameron kept up a steady swift walking pace, but Michael, determined to give it his all, jogged up and down the aisles. When Cameron finally tracked Michael down to explain that the contest was over (he'd won), he found Michael, sweat dripping off his forehead, still seeking out products.

Later that night at his motel, Michael reflected on the real worth of what he'd learned, not just from Cameron but also from his other undercover experiences. "I grew up with successful, supportive parents who set great examples for me, and who helped me develop and be a better person. Cameron had none of that, but he's doing it himself for his daughter. Meeting someone like him and seeing the magic between him and his daughter put a real face to the idea that life is so much more than business. It made me want to get home and give my own daughter lots of hugs."

Putting all his undercover experiences into perspective, Michael realized that the primary lessons he'd learned hadn't been about improving efficiency; they'd been about looking for the balance between work and life. "It would be unfair of me to say that I really understand what all the people I'd worked with are going through. We work for different reasons. I work because I have an absolute love for business. They work because they need to provide for their families. I put so much effort into GSI Commerce that it takes away from other things. I'm a good husband, but I could be a better husband. I'm a good father, but I could be a great father. The most valuable lesson I got from spending time undercover was about how I could be a better person."

HE REVEALS THE TRUTH

After giving his daughter those much anticipated hugs on arriving home, Michael scheduled meetings with all his coworkers from the prior week at GSI's headquarters outside Philadelphia. None were aware of why they had been called to the home office. They certainly weren't prepared for what was waiting for them.

A remarkably composed Rashelle instantly recognized "the seasonal" when he came in the door. Her response after learning "Gary's" true identity was to jokingly (if nervously) ask if she was fired, as well as to ask if Michael was tired the day after they worked together. "You gave me the most unbelievable workout of my life," Michael readily admitted. "Watching how hard you worked, and how well you represented the company after only being with us for three weeks, made me very proud. I'd like to offer you a full-time job with benefits. We'd be honored to have you on our team." Rashelle instantly accepted, saying she'd love to work with Michael at GSI, "and be part of something so absolutely wonderful."

An uncomfortable Cameron responded with a knowing but nervous smile when he saw his picking competitor walk in the office door. The smile remained, but the nervousness faded when Michael explained who he was, and described his undercover experience. "You're a hardworking guy, with great energy about you. You do an incredible job," Michael began. "But what really struck me was seeing you with your daughter. I want to help you have a better Christmas, so we'd like to give you a $1,000 gift card so you can do some great shopping for her." Cameron's eyes welled up with tears. "With your winning attitude, you're a potential leader and a manager. As of today, we're putting you in a training program to get you on a fast track to become a supervisor."

Shannon broke out in embarrassed laughter when Michael entered the office and revealed his true identity. She grew even more discomfited by the praise heaped upon her. "To see how hard you work, with such pride, was an inspiration to me. I want to work just as hard to make GSI a better company. It's people like you who make us so successful." As tears flowed down Shannon's cheeks, Michael revealed that the company was donating $5,000 toward her sons' football teams, to make up for her not being able to spend time fundraising for them. Shannon choked up at the unexpected gratification of having the CEO experience what her job was like and listen to her, and then step up and do something for a cause she cared about.

Danielle's confidence deserted her when Michael revealed who he was. He'd been eager to speak with her since the incident, and although his anger had softened, his vehemence had not. Recounting the situation, Michael stressed that "the way that call was handled was unacceptable. That's not the way we treat customers." Danielle rationalized the incident, citing her scant training and recent transfer to escalations. Accepting that those were factors and that the company bore some responsibility, Michael still insisted "that's no excuse to be rude to a customer." Danielle accepted that she could have handled the situation better and professed her readiness to learn from the experience and further training.

Adam greeted with a broad grin the news that his trainee was actually his CEO, and he humbly acknowledged Michael's praise for his skill and performance. Adam's face tightened with emotion as the conversation turned personal. "Listening to your story broke my heart," Michael related. "I was ready for a lot of things when I went undercover, but I would be full of it if I said I was remotely prepared for what you told me. One of the things you talked about was saving money to get married, so I'd like to put $10,000 toward your wedding." Stunned that the CEO was willing to do that for him, Adam again demonstrated his gift for putting things in perspective. "It really goes to show you that a positive attitude will bring good things to your life, and that karma really does exist."

Michael also looked to put his chance connection with Adam into a broader context. "With 10,000 people working for us during peak season, you're bound to hear about tragedies. But usually it's through an e-mail. You feel terrible and you make a donation, but it's not the same as when you're there, speaking with someone, face-to-face. That connection makes the feeling far more profound and real." Even for an entrepreneur whose work has always been his life, there are times when the personal transcends the professional.

Another such moment arose when, having finished his one-on-one meetings with his undercover coworkers, Michael addressed the entire staff in the company auditorium, where his presentation would be beamed by teleconference to its other locations. After sharing the video of all the most embarrassing moments of his experiences, a new Michael Rubin appeared on stage. The high-energy, fast-talking, business-obsessed entrepreneur had been replaced by a more introspective, emotional leader. "As the founder of the company, you can become a little bit removed from people," he confessed. "I've been focused on growing the company. I now realize I need to put more energy into improving our policies and our systems to create a better environment for all of you. This experience has really touched my heart, as both a manager and a man."

With the applause and hoopla finished, Michael had yet another epiphany. "Going undercover made me realize that I've got an incredible family and an amazing daughter. Life's precious. It's short. You need to strike a balance. This experience convinced me to focus not just on accomplishing business results but also on accomplishing human results: touching people one by one."

SINCE THE SHOW

★ **Rashelle** now has a full-time position, with benefits, at GSI. Having been trained in 12 different positions, she is proving to be as valuable an addition to the team as Michael had anticipated. She recently had reason to be grateful for her new medical benefits, having broken her hand going down a water slide.

★ **Cameron** completed training and attended a recent GSI leadership conference that put him on the fast track to becoming a supervisor. However, he's passed up on the actual promotion for now because it would have meant leapfrogging over someone who had worked longer for the company.

★ **Shannon** is still one of the company's premier packers. Her sons' football teams are the best dressed in their leagues.

★ **Danielle** went back for retraining, but is no longer with GSI. "I had a chance to spend time with Danielle after this experience," Michael revealed. "She's a good person who simply isn't cut out for this job. It happens."

★ **Adam** moved from Florida and is now working at GSI's corporate headquarters outside Philadelphia, in a new role with greater responsibilities. He and his fiancée are planning their wedding—and he's getting used to being asked for his autograph.

★ **Michael** is still Founder and CEO of GSI Commerce. He didn't take offense to the portrayal as a workaholic entrepreneur "because it's true." But he is working on it. "My daughter and I have a better relationship today than we did when the show was taped because she has grown, and I've learned there's more to life than just business." He came away from going undercover with even more enthusiasm for his company. "If there was one thing that really exceeded my expectations, it was how incredibly good our hourly workers are at very difficult jobs, and how motivated they are to excel. I am more charged up than ever about creating opportunities to grow the company for our people, and about creating an even better environment for them and their families." He's become a firm believer in executives taking time to go out into the field. "It was a great experience. If you're going to go undercover in your own business, you need to fully immerse yourself in the experience. I'm going to try to go undercover again during our next peak season . . . but this time, without the cameras."

WHAT RICHES CAN'T BUY

"We believe leadership has three prongs: financial performance, making the company a great place for great people to work, and practicing servant leadership."

Joel Manby
CEO, Herschend Family

John Briggs
New Employee

How We Found the Boss

Each year hundreds of millions of visitors crowd through the gates of America's amusement parks. The industry employs approximately 500,000 year-round and seasonal employees. And we were eager to take viewers inside the inner workings of one of these operations for an episode of Undercover Boss. Herschend Family Entertainment struck us as especially suitable because of their numerous and varied properties and their promotion of family values. We were glad to discover Herschend led by a thoughtful and charismatic boss. A rather unique career path led CEO Joel Manby to his position at the helm of the Herschend family's amusement park businesses. As he never worked at the parks before becoming CEO, he leapt at the chance to go back and start on the shop floor.

THE BOSS

Joel Manby, president and CEO.

HIS COVER

John Briggs, a new recruit to the company who's been laid off from the auto industry, and is being followed by a TV crew documenting entry-level jobs at HFE.

HIS COMPANY

In an industry dominated by giant corporations, Herschend Family Entertainment (HFE) remains very much a family business. It was founded by Hugo and Mary Herschend, who fell in love with the Missouri Ozarks during a family vacation with sons Jack and Pete in 1950. The metro Atlanta–based company's stated mission is to "Create Memories Worth Repeating" for more than 14 million guests who visit its 22 properties annually. HFE has more than 10,000 employees dedicated to that mission and reaps $300 million in annual revenue as its reward. Among the company's properties in the Branson, Missouri, area are Silver Dollar City, Marvel Cave, White Water Branson, the Showboat Branson Belle riverboat, and Talking Rocks Cavern. The company has a long-term lease to operate Stone Mountain Park in Atlanta, and owns the nearby Crossroads Village, Wild Adventures theme park, and Splash Island Water Park. HFE also owns aquariums in Newport, Kentucky, and Camden, New Jersey; Ride the Ducks amphibious tour rides in Branson, Newport, Philadelphia, Stone Mountain, Seattle, and San Francisco; and Classic Cable Car Sightseeing, also in San Francisco.

HIS STORY

HFE openly embraces servant leadership, defining it as a code of behavior consistent with Christian values and ethics that involves patience, kindness, honesty, humility, respect, selflessness, commitment, and forgiveness. The Herschend family believes that if the company treats its employees according to these principles, those employees will treat their guests the same way. Joel Manby is charged with putting these principles into practice.

One might think paying it forward is just an abstraction for Joel, who appears to have led a charmed life. Tall and good looking, he has a beautiful wife and four lovely daughters, one adopted from China. As president and CEO of HFE, he makes an excellent living. Joel was a valedictorian and sports star at tiny Albion College, as well as a Rhodes Scholarship finalist. He received his master's from the Harvard Business School and rose through the ranks in the auto industry to become the youngest head of an automaker, when he was named CEO of Saab USA at age 35. But Joel's impressive success actually has very humble origins.

Born into a working-class family in Battle Creek, Michigan, Joel and his two brothers shared the sole bedroom in the tiny house, while his parents slept in the kitchen. "My father worked like crazy, but never seemed to catch a break," Joel remembered. After losing his farm machinery dealership, Joel's father worked in an auto factory, and when he came home went to work mowing lawns, plowing fields, and clearing snow. That meant he missed all of Joel's sports successes. One in particular stands out. "My father didn't see me hit a grand slam to win the local Little League championship. Then my mom told me I couldn't go to the team party afterwards because we didn't have the money for a soda at A&W." Joel, a standout student and athlete, was only able to go to Albion because local philanthropist George Markham, owner of Archway Cookies, paid his tuition.

Joel's hard work and determination led to a stellar college career. He was accepted to Harvard Business School for his graduate degree but once again, he couldn't afford the tuition. So Joel deferred his acceptance and took an entry-level job at General Motors with the ambition of winning one of the automaker's Sloan Fellowships, which would not only pay his tuition, but fifty percent of his salary as well. After just two years on the job, Joel had won the award.

Graduating from Harvard, Joel fulfilled the terms of his fellowship by returning to General Motors. He rose through the corporate ranks quickly, and was recruited to join the launch team for Saturn, GM's effort at creating "a different kind of car company," designed to compete with low-cost imports. Having achieved financial stability, Joel approached his hometown benefactor and offered to repay the cost of his undergraduate tuition. But George Markham told him to instead make the same generous contribution to the education of another struggling young person. And Joel did.

Joel was a key contributor in helping to grow Saturn's sales to $5 billion within five years. He rose to the number two spot at the Tennessee-based automaker and was then asked by GM to run Saab USA, which they owned. Joel moved his family to Georgia, to take up his position at Saab USA headquarters, becoming the youngest CEO of an automaker.

As the 1990s drew to a close and at the height of the dot.com boom, Joel was once again recruited to a prestigious post in the auto industry. Greenlight.com, an online car buying service that bought cars from dealers for resale to online customers, had been founded by the impressive partnership of Amazon.com and Silicon Valley's top venture capital firms. Joel couldn't resist the promise of dot.com dollars and the challenge of stewarding this new enterprise. In April 2000, he left Saturn to become Greenlight's president. Joel's timing couldn't have been worse.

No sooner had Joel signed on with Greenlight, the dot .com stock bubble burst. In his first week at the new company, the NASDAQ stock index plunged 30 percent. Rather than taking command of a rocket bound for blast off, Joel found himself at the helm of a sinking ship. Joel worked around the clock at the company's San Francisco headquarters while his family remained behind in Georgia. Lonely and under extreme pressure to cut jobs and salvage some aspect of the enterprise, he fell into a depression, often employing alcohol as a sleep aid. Instead of securing his family's financial future with the move to Greenlight, suddenly the marriage he prized above anything was at risk. In the nick of time, Joel was able to negotiate the sale of Greenlight to Carsdirect.com, enabling him to return home.

After a life of overcoming obstacles and succeeding, Joel had suffered not just a business failure but a personal failure as well. Shortly after returning home, Joel experienced an epiphany during a sermon at his church. Realizing that he had traded happiness with his wife and children in exchange for career success, Joel committed to always putting his family first. "(Approach) work as a marathon, not (as) a sprint." It was at this point, in 2003, when he was at his lowest both professionally and personally, that a helping hand reached out: HFE's owners asked Joel to take over as CEO.

> *"It's been wonderful to be in a position where there's no disconnect between my work and personal values."*

It was a match made in heaven. "It's been wonderful to be in a position where there's no disconnect between my work and personal values," Joel affirmed. "We believe leadership has three prongs: financial performance, making the company a great place for great people to work, and practicing servant leadership." His family is happier than ever. With Joel at the helm, HFE has expanded to become the tenth-largest family entertainment and theme park company in the world, moving to the top tier of an industry that is dominated by much larger international, publicly held companies, such as Disney, Universal, Six Flags, and Anheuser-Busch.

"I hadn't been getting out as much as I used to before the economic downturn, partly because I'd been so busy dealing with the financial situation. But in hindsight, I also think I was a little sheepish because of having to make all the cuts. I realized I needed to get out there and see how our people were doing and if they still felt good about the company."

The company has worked hard to maintain its values-driven culture, but the recent economic downturn has made that difficult: since the end of 2008, customers have been cutting back their entertainment spending. In response, in 2009 HFE had to make cuts. "We have millions of dollars invested in facilities. We have to be profitable or the whole enterprise will collapse, and then all the jobs would go away." There were layoffs in areas where anticipated growth failed to materialize. Wages were frozen. Benefits were cut, and there were no raises. Although these measures were across the board, they were most painful for the company's frontline personnel. Many of these employees work seasonally and were already living paycheck to paycheck. "It was a real test for us because it's tough to make cuts when you're always trying to talk about servant leadership."

Joel decided to go undercover in order to see how the company's culture had fared in light of the cutbacks. He was also feeling a bit guilty. "I hadn't been getting out as much as I used to before the economic downturn," Joel admitted, "partly because I'd been so busy dealing with the financial situation. But in hindsight, I also think I was a little sheepish because of having to make all the cuts. I realized I needed to get out there and see how our people were doing and if they still felt good about the company. I wanted to do it undercover so I'd get the unvarnished truth. When people know you're the CEO, they always treat you a little differently." Joel also wanted to make sure that the guest experience, so central to HFE's present and future success, hadn't suffered due to belt tightening or reduced enthusiasm. With faith and a bit of trepidation, he left the corporate office and headed out into the field.

JOB #1

Qwacking the Code

Ride the Ducks Crew, Stone Mountain GA

Beginning their lives as U.S. Army amphibious trucks in World War II, Herschend's Ride the Ducks have been modernized and transformed into floating tour buses. The open-air vehicles drive around town on a rolling tour of local sites until they slowly take to the water to continue the tour afloat. They can be found from San Francisco to Philadelphia, but one thing they all share is that the captain is vital in making sure the customer has a good time. "The Duck captain isn't part of the experience; he *is* the experience," Joel explained. This is the last position where the company could afford a drop in morale and enthusiasm. Joel chose to visit the Ride the Ducks operation at Atlanta's Stone Mountain Park, which is Georgia's number one attraction.

Joel's boss for the day was Captain Howard, a giant of a man with a ducklike walk and the ironic nickname of Tiny. With total professionalism, Captain Howard introduced Joel to the rudiments of the job and safety features of the vehicle. He explained that balancing safety with entertainment is what makes the captain's job so important. The captain needed to put on a show, but also needed to be aware that taking children out on the water was a great responsibility. Captain Howard advised the newbie to study him carefully because fun on the duck boat was "serious stuff."

The fun started upon boarding, with Captain Howard and Joel fitting the young patrons with life jackets, asking each child his or her name, giving the kids big smiles and telling them to make sure to get a "qwacker" noisemaker. The otherwise warm and mild Captain Howard transformed into a living cartoon character for his guests. Climbing up the rear ramp of the amphibian, Captain Howard had an ear-to-ear grin and began bouncing from side to side on his feet, rocking the massive vehicle, announcing "little fella coming through." With the children still laughing, Captain Howard waddled down the aisle and plopped into his "cockpit." After giving brief (and often hilarious) descriptions of sights as they passed, Captain Howard got the kids revved up for the ultimate Duck boat moment: their entry into the placid lake. He told them not to worry and assured them that he himself was a floatation device. He then had the kids put their hands in the air and shout "Go, Captain, go!" as he drove the vehicle into the water. Once they were under way, Captain Howard's family-friendly jokes and funny faces kept the children engaged and laughing for the duration of the trip.

Joel was amazed at the incongruous mix of personas the corpulent captain could project: informative tour guide, skilled driver and skipper, and goofy children's entertainer. Watching Captain Howard pull off this trifecta, seamlessly shifting between roles depending on the audience and situation, was a revelation for someone as even-tempered as Joel. After a while, the "Duck-in-training" gave up trying to be anything other than a straight man for the star of the show. Joel was convinced he'd found the model for what a Duck captain should be.

JOB #2

The Future of HFE

Entrance Person-in-Charge, Silver Dollar City, Branson MO

Silver Dollar City, a theme park based on life in the 1880s, has earned its reputation as the nation's friendliest attraction. Joel's undercover assignment would take him to the front gate, where guests' first impressions of the park's hospitality were formed.

The period costume worn by Albert, Joel's trainer for the day, couldn't disguise his youth or his 21st-century hyperactivity.

"Energy and passion can sometimes be overwhelming, but you'd rather have someone like that, with whom maybe you have to pull back on the reins, than someone with whom you have to use the spurs."

Albert, 21, had been working at Silver Dollar City in one capacity or another since he was 14. The job has been an economic lifeline for his family, enabling Albert to help out his parents, a waitress and a teacher.

Outfitted in his own period costume, Joel was set up at one of the turnstiles at the park's entrance. Albert demonstrated the job, showing off his gift for making everyone arriving feel like a special guest, while still getting bodies through the turnstiles at an efficient clip. Joel, whose biggest fear about going undercover had been spoiling a guest's experience, found the job thrilling. Welcoming the smiling customers was the best medicine for a CEO who'd been worried about the customer experience.

Later, as they got to know each other over break, Albert explained that the theme park industry is his passion, and that Silver Dollar City is not just another place to work. It didn't take much encouragement from Joel for Albert to pull out his laptop computer and demonstrate his design for an underwater roller coaster. As the two chatted, Albert explained that he was working full-time at the park while also going to college at night. Albert was not shy about stating his ultimate career goal: to become CEO of Herschend (although he did acknowledge that he'd heard that the man who had the job now was "an awesome guy").

After a day spent trying to keep up with his ebullient future replacement, Joel felt that Albert's enthusiasm was just what the company needed, especially in tough times. "Albert's energy and passion can sometimes be overwhelming, but you'd rather have someone like that, with whom maybe you have to pull back on the reins, than someone with whom you have to use the spurs," Joel explained, using the vernacular of Silver Dollar City. Joel confessed he saw more than a little of himself in the intense and ambitious Albert. "I grew up poor, like he did. And I was aggressive and motivated. The difference was I got a few breaks along the way."

JOB #3

A Wake-Up Call

Street Washer, Silver Dollar City, Branson MO

Besides being known as the friendliest theme park in the country, Silver Dollar City has been ranked as the cleanest park in America, and Joel was going to get a predawn lesson in how that distinction is earned.

Richard, Joel's boss for the day, warned him they'd be in for a busy morning. A 12-year veteran of cleanup work at Silver Dollar City, Richard works the early predawn shift in order to spend more time with his family.

Handling and maneuvering the high-pressure hose with the skill of a firefighter, Richard washed down the walkways in front of some of the food shops, quickly leaving them spotless. Richard coached the newbie on how to quickly stem the water

flow by making a kink in the hose and then stepping on it, the way you'd play a prank on someone who was watering the lawn. Joel was less than adept at the chore when he took over, doing a better job at hosing down Richard than the sidewalks. In an effort to get the job done in time and keep from getting drenched, Richard had to reclaim control of the hose.

With Joel now relegated to observer, and able to focus for the first time on the employee training him, he asked Richard about himself and learned that they shared in common being adoptive parents. Richard and his wife have three sons of their own. But they felt their family was not complete without a girl. During the adoption process, they learned that the little girl they had their sights on had a sister as well. They decided it wouldn't be right to separate the little girls, so they adopted them both. Richard confessed to Joel that times were hard now for Richard's family, as they had lost their home in a flood and were still in the process of repairing the house. HFE has a financial assistance program for employees, designed to help with just this kind of catastrophic need, but after some subtle questioning, Joel learned that Richard hadn't applied for help.

Richard's tale brought back memories of Joel's father's struggles. "Richard has such a big heart, and is such a great family man. He doesn't make a lot of money, works so hard, then gets hit with a financial catastrophe, but doesn't complain or blame the world. He just does what he has to." Joel was frustrated that Richard hadn't applied for help from the company and decided then and there to encourage Richard to accept help from HFE. "The money is there. We want it to be used. I know Richard's a proud man. But we can't help him and we can't help others if they don't apply."

JOB #4

Riverboat Gamblers

Food Server, Showboat Branson Belle, Branson MO

Joel's fear of diminishing a guest's experience was at its peak at his next job. He would be waiting on tables on the Showboat Branson Belle and was petrified he'd dump the contents of a tray on a customer's lap. The boat is a replica 1800s riverboat, custom-built on the site as a lake-going showboat that can handle 700 passengers. The boat's 1994 launch party attracted national attention when in order to avoid using grease or oil that would pollute the waters of Table Rock Lake, HFE used two tons of bananas to lubricate the launching rails. Joel prayed there would be no banana peels on the dining room floor.

The showboat experience is its unique dinner theater. Multi-course meals are served during stage shows—while the boat is moving—and must be strictly timed, requiring precise coordination among the crew, kitchen personnel, serving staff, and entertainers. Poor morale can easily result in slip-ups, interfering with the guest experience. At a time when attendance is already down due to the poor economy, a decline in service is the last thing the company needs.

For his shift as a waiter in the main dining room, Joel would train under Jennifer, a vivacious 30-year-old brunette, who was momentarily dismayed to learn that "John" had never waited on tables before. For better or worse, there was no time to be anxious. Dressed in his period waiter's costume, Joel did his best to keep from fouling up the carefully timed choreography of the meal service. The huge trays each balanced nine servings, and whereas the experienced staff hoisted them with one hand in a dramatic entrance parade, Joel needed two for balance as well as his shoulder to keep them from crashing down. Soon he was sweating from fear as well as from the hard work. Jennifer, in contrast, was a master of friendly efficiency. Joel needn't have worried about how he'd do. The retired ladies who made up the majority of his customers were thrilled by his close attention, not particularly caring that he had no waiting skills. As Joel and Jennifer wrapped up their first shift, chatting with customers as they cleared, "John" was held back by more than a few of the ladies, who slipped him some extra tips. "The ladies think he's adorable," Jennifer confided with a laugh.

PRODUCERS' NOTE
What You Didn't See

Joel managed to hang on to a physical souvenir from each job he performed on *Undercover Boss*—the uniform from each position. From the colonial garb he wore with Albert to the tuxedo he donned with Jennifer, Joel has them all hung up in his closet at home. And, of course, he formed a strong attachment to the jean jacket that came to define John Briggs, his undercover persona. But Joel kept his clothes for a deeper reason than just adding a couple of fancy outfits to his wardrobe: he wanted to continue the *Undercover Boss* experience, even after the cameras had stopped rolling. Even though some are likely to recognize him at the parks, whether he wears his authentic uniform or a more traditional suit and tie, Joel wants to relive the amazing connections he had with his employees and always keep the lessons he learned in mind.

Up on deck for their break, Jennifer received a call from her babysitter that one of her daughters was ill. Concerned, Joel asked about Jennifer's family and learned she was a single mother with two daughters, ages ten and seven. Jennifer explained how difficult it was for employees like her, who don't work nine to five, to get child care. But more frustrating, she revealed, was that with attendance down, servers are often rotated into empty stations and sent home. That's doubly difficult, she noted: on those evenings, she not only goes unpaid but also still has to pay her babysitter for the time she is away. "This job is a gamble," Jennifer said with obvious worry. "You never know that's going to happen when you come in."

Joel admitted he hadn't realized the extent of the problem Jennifer was facing. "We'd always thought of our seasonal employees as being primarily empty nesters, so our focus has been on health care rather than child care," he explained. "But I've seen that we have far more single moms working for us than I realized. We ought to have some kind of assistance for them," he opined. "What can be more catastrophic on a daily basis for a single parent than a child-care issue?"

JOB #5

A Touching Story

Odd Jobber, Adventure Aquarium, Camden NJ

On his final day undercover, Joel worked in one of HFE's newest acquisitions, the Adventure Aquarium, just outside Philadelphia. Joel explained, "I haven't had a chance to get to know these people or this attraction yet. I've heard it's a very

concentrated experience, with lots of kids in a small area, and that they do a good job handling that combination. I want to learn how they manage it."

Led up a staircase crowded with preteen children, Joel discovered an even larger crowd of buzzing kids swarming around what was to be his post, the "touch tank"—a large open aquarium where children, with the assistance of a trainer, can pick up and touch various sea creatures. Mercedes, a vivacious 25-year-old and Joel's trainer, wasted no time prepping him and instead urged him to dive on in. With charm and charisma, she taught the children (and Joel!) the different species in the tank.

Detecting a lull in the activity only an expert could spot, Mercedes sized the opportunity to introduce Joel to the next of their shared responsibilities: cleaning. Spray bottles and cloths in hand, Mercedes showed Joel how to quickly clean the large aquarium glass, which was cloudy with young handprints, while navigating around the children. "Speedy, speedy, speedy," she encouraged with a huge smile. Pointing out smudges he missed and urging him to put some muscle into his work, a determined but still chipper Mercedes rhetorically asked, "Have you ever done cleaning like this?" When Joel laughed in frustration, pointing out that no sooner had he finished cleaning when another child would cover the glass with fresh smudgy fingerprints, Mercedes just said, "No excuses, no excuses."

Impressed with Mercedes's dedication and energy, Joel asked about her other responsibilities. "I also work in accounting and finance, and I do events hosting—pretty much a little bit of everything." Mercedes explained that she had been working at the aquarium for two years, and that before she got the job she and her son were homeless. Mercedes's son was only one year old at the time, and they were forced to sleep on the floor of his daycare center because she couldn't find a job. "So once I got the job here I've just been saying 'yes' to everything and accepting every opportunity this place has to offer. I think the more you know, the better," she explained, adding with a laugh, "the pay comes later."

At the end of the day, sitting outside the aquarium, Joel was still moved by his talk with Mercedes. "It was really humbling to hear what she's been through and to see the attitude she has now. What an amazing person. I had such a loving home and my parents were such a support mechanism for me, and she's had to go through all this on her own. We have a program to help people like her, and like Richard, but they didn't apply. It just means we have to do something to make sure our people access that money. Every dollar that's left in that fund at the end of the year isn't a dollar saved; it's a lost opportunity to help someone in need."

Reflecting upon his week undercover, an exhausted Joel spoke about the experience in philosophical terms. "You see so much pain and you ask, 'Why does it have to be like this?'" Choking up, he recalled something Albert had said, about how HFE was like a family. "That's true. The Herschends see everyone who works for them as part of their family. Profits are important because we have to grow the company and keep everyone employed, but that shouldn't be the only thing that drives every decision. Of all the times for my heart to grow bigger, in the middle of one of the worst recessions in our history probably wasn't a good time," he joked. "This is going to make all of our decisions tougher, but that's what leadership is all about."

> "Profits are important because we have to grow the company and keep everyone employed, but that shouldn't be the only thing that drives every decision. Of all the times for my heart to grow bigger, in the middle of one of the worst recessions in our history probably wasn't a good time," he joked. "This is going to make all of our decisions tougher, but that's what leadership is all about."

HE REVEALS THE TRUTH

Meeting with his leadership team back at headquarters, Joel revealed that there was one overriding issue they faced. "We have financial assistance for our employees. And almost without fail, the people I talked to and worked with had not applied for it even when they had huge needs." The executive committee was stunned and puzzled. They questioned if it was a communications problem—that the employees were unaware of what was available. Joel explained that it was due not to a lack of information but to an abundance of pride. "No one wants to apply for financial assistance," he stated simply. "We have got to figure out how to market the program better and get more people to apply."

Joel then turned to his second major discovery. "We have to find a way to serve single parents better. They are a larger part of our workforce than we'd realized, and we need to help them meet their challenges." Joel charged his team to reach out to their own people with an open mind as to how they could address this pressing need.

Having given his marching orders to his executives, Joel left the conference room to meet with his "bosses" from the prior week. Each had been brought to headquarters without being told the reason for the trip.

The moment Captain Howard saw his "Duck-in-training" enter the office, he broke out into a huge grin and greeted "John" warmly. When he learned whom he'd taken under his wing, he was shocked. "You're my boss's boss?" he asked incredulously. Joel explained that he'd never seen someone able to transform himself the way Captain Howard did on the tour. "I tried to interact with the kids, but you, in some sense, became a kid. I asked myself, 'Can we take some of Captain Howard's magic and put it at other Ride the Duck tours in other locations?' I'd like for you to be able to go to these other cities and teach them some of what you do." "I'm there," Captain Howard promised with a bear hug.

Jennifer was concerned to be face-to-face with the CEO, worried that her earlier comments would get her into trouble. But Joel's patient manner soon put her at ease. Relaying how impressed he was with her work ethic, Joel admitted that what Jennifer did for him was to put a face to being a single parent. He told her that the company was expanding its financial assistance program to include child care, so she could take that worry out of her life. Smiling she said, "It's the one thing I struggle most with, so it feels amazing to not have to worry about it so much."

Richard's jaw literally dropped when Joel revealed his true identity. Shaking his head, all he could say was "You got me." Telling Richard that he was a special man and that the company was lucky to have him as an employee, Joel explained that the company was going to allocate $10,000 in catastrophic aid to help him repair his home, and that a group of company employees—including Joel—would come to the site to help him get

PRODUCERS' NOTE
What You Didn't See

Because of the shooting schedule of this episode, we ended up filming the finale on Halloween. Although nobody came to the speeches or the one-on-one interviews in full costume, everyone was keenly aware of the date and the time of day, especially the parents whose kids were looking forward to trick-or-treating that night.

Once we wrapped up the festivities in Atlanta, the contributors headed to the airport to embark on the flights our production team had booked for them. But Joel had something better in store. Not content with sending his employees home on commercial flights, Joel gathered them all together and put them on a private jet so they could get home in time to be with their families on Halloween.

the work done sooner than he could do it himself. "I never dreamed something like this could happen," the stunned street cleaner acknowledged. "It's going to be a big relief."

Mercedes laughed with embarrassment when Joel entered and told her who she'd coached on glass-cleaning technique. Saying that he thought she was an incredible worker with an amazing attitude, Joel told her that he was giving her an immediate raise. With a tearful Mercedes listening in disbelief, Joel went on to say that to honor her rising out of being homeless, HFE would help her put together an inventory of everything she needed for her apartment, and would then take care of the cost. "I hope you're with our company for a long time," Joel stressed. "Who knows—maybe we'll get to see you move into a home of your own one day." All Mercedes could say was, "I feel like I'm on top of the world."

"In the middle of a historic economic downturn, I went to the general managers of our properties, our CFO, our board, and our owners, and asked them to spend more money on our people. And the response of every single person was excitement at the chance."

Albert, the 21-year-old ball of energy with designs on Joel's job, instantly recognized his trainee and jumped to his feet to shake hands when Joel walked into the office. When he learned whom he was meeting, he laughed. Joel told the earnest

Albert that his working full-time and going to school at the same time inspired the CEO to start a scholarship program, and that Albert would be the first recipient. "You're going to get to go to school full-time so you don't have to work all day," Joel explained as Albert began choking up. "We're going to also pay you your 40-hour-a-week salary while you go to school," Joel continued. At the news Albert broke down, sobbing, and for the first time he was speechless. "All we ask is that in the summertime, when you're not going to school full-time, you come back to work," Joel concluded. Before Joel could even finish his sentence, Albert said he'd love to. "The first thing I'm going to do now is call my parents," Albert announced, the tears coming once again. "I know they're going to be so proud."

Having spoken with all of his coworkers from his undercover week, Joel then addressed a gathering of company staff. After showing them video clips of his week, and laughing along at his clumsy missteps and failings, Joel turned serious. "We talk a lot about creating a great guest experience, but I had no idea how great you guys are and how passionate you are about your jobs, about each other, and about the company. I have a renewed respect and appreciation for what you all do on the front line. I could not be more proud of you."

Joel's thoughts turned to the pride he felt in working for his company. "In the middle of a historic economic downturn, I went to the general managers of our properties, our CFO, our board, and our owners, and asked them to spend more money on our people. And the response of every single person was excitement at the chance. Most people want to work for more than money. They want to work for a cause, for a company that cares about other people, the environment, and their community. In business we get focused on the bottom line and what we have to do to satisfy our shareholders. I'm so lucky to be in a position to help people who are down on their luck, and to work for a company that believes in helping our fellow man."

Going undercover had given Joel an opportunity to make sure that even in difficult economic times, his company could continue to adhere to its founding Christian principles. It had also given him a chance to demonstrate his own values, and a chance to repay the individuals and organizations who had helped him when he was in need. It gave him a chance to pay it forward.

SINCE THE SHOW

* **Captain Howard** has been sharing his techniques and ideas with his peers in other cities around the country in HFE's new Captain's Program.

* **Jennifer** is now getting almost as much attention from her customers as Joel did. Thanks to the company's new single-parent assistance program, she has her child-care costs covered. HFE's program offers $100 per child per month payments, up to a total of $300 per month per employee, for child-care expenses for single parents whose income is at or below 185 percent of the local poverty level. Because only about 50 of the approximately 250 qualifying employees have applied for the assistance, Joel and the rest of the executives are trying to come up with ways to encourage greater participation. There's also discussion to expand the program to include two-parent families as well.

★ **Mercedes** received her raise and furnishings that helped turn her apartment into a home for her and her son.

★ HFE paid for the repairs to **Richard's** home, and even added another bathroom onto the house in the process. While working on Richard's home, HFE realized that its existing $10,000 ceiling for catastrophic assistance wasn't sufficient. The company has now doubled the maximum amount to $20,000.

★ **Albert** got married, and he and his new wife moved to Valdosta, Georgia, where he'll be attending college full-time and working for the company during the summer. The company has decided to change the terms of the new scholarship program. Rather than giving one recipient full tuition plus an income, the company will in future provide full tuition to three recipients. Albert, however, will keep getting his salary plus tuition as long as he maintains a 3.0 grade-point average.

★ **Joel** remains CEO of Herschend Family Entertainment. His undercover experience has reaffirmed some of his core beliefs that might have otherwise been obscured by the economic downturn. "There's a simple business principle to which I adhere: the level of enthusiasm of the guest experience can never rise higher than the enthusiasm of your own employees. Going undercover reminded me of that. In the total scheme of things, all the new programs we've added don't add up to big dollars. Yet they've made our already dedicated employees even more enthusiastic at a time when morale could be down. We've outperformed every other regional theme park company, and I believe that's at least partly due to our putting our principles and values into practice." Since his undercover experience, the quiet CEO has been more aggressive about sharing HFE's principles. "I'm less reticent now and have become more outspoken. It was scary to go undercover, but it was one of the best decisions I ever made. It's truly a great feeling to help people."

TROUBLES DOWN THE DRAIN

"The title and trappings of the corner office are always barriers to totally honest communication. It's so easy to make a decision in a vacuum and then send out a company-wide e-mail or make some announcement in a corporate newsletter."

Rick Arquilla
COO, Roto-Rooter

Hank Denman
New Employee

How We Found the Boss

We were immediately attracted to Roto-Rooter because of the direct interface its employees have with their customers. Many companies attract people to their stores, but there are relatively few iconic American brands that still send workers directly into their customers' homes. When we met the boss for his casting interview, Rick's sincere and open personality sealed the deal. Rick knew that this undercover experience would require him to literally roll up his sleeves and get his hands dirty. And he was game for the challenge.

THE BOSS

Rick Arquilla, president and COO.

HIS COVER

Hank Denman, a new recruit to the company being filmed for a video about the company's 75th anniversary.

HIS COMPANY

It was in the late 1920s that Samuel Blanc decided to do something about a stubborn drain in his son Milton's Des Moines, Iowa, apartment. Frustrated at their inability to fix the problem without having to dig up lawns to reach the buried sewer lines, Samuel and his son combined a washing machine motor, roller skate wheels, and a steel cable, and built a machine whose sharp rotating blades could cut tree roots that had grown through pipes and clogged lines, without having to dig. Samuel's wife, Lettie, dubbed the invention the Roto-Rooter. Sales of the machine took off, because it represented an easy-entry entrepreneurial effort in the midst of the Great Depression. Seventy-five years later, Roto-Rooter, now headquartered in Cincinnati, is the largest provider of plumbing and drain cleaning services in North America, operating businesses in 110 company-owned territories and 500 franchisee-owned territories. Franchises have also been established in Japan, the Philippines, Australia, the United Kingdom, Indonesia, and Singapore. The company employs more than 7,000 people, who help it generate annual sales of more than $700 million. Although still primarily associated with drain cleaning, Roto-Rooter technicians are full-service plumbers, doing everything from installing toilets to repairing leaking faucets. The company also offers 24/7 emergency service in many of the areas it serves.

HIS STORY

Heroism is too often equated with stoicism. Silence, distance, and emotional reserve can often be perceived as strength of character. Any boss—any person—will tell you that being emotionally open, making oneself vulnerable, requires not only bravery but also a real strength of character.

Rick Arquilla would never call himself heroic—that's not how he was raised. Rick grew up in the small town of Mt. Vernon, Ohio, where everyone's father was either a farmer or a factory worker. Although he's never forgotten his roots, he was encouraged to transcend them. Rick's parents routinely made him promise to go to college so that he wouldn't follow in his father's footsteps as a factory worker. He fulfilled his commitment to his folks, graduating from The Ohio State University and entering the business world wearing a white collar.

"A young man came to me recently and asked for the secret of my success . . . all I could tell him was to work really hard every day, and when you catch one or two breaks, make the most of them."

Working his way up corporate ladders, Rick joined Chemlawn, and was eventually named a vice president of that firm. He credits hard work and determination for his eventually being named president and COO of Roto-Rooter in 1999. "A young man came to me recently and asked for the secret of my success," Rick recalled. "I know he wanted me to give him some formula, but all I could tell him was to work really hard every day, and when you catch one or two breaks, make the most of them."

It's not just Rick who's made the most of his breaks. Roto-Rooter has benefitted as well. Under Rick's leadership, the company expanded beyond its traditional drain cleaning specialty to offer a full range of residential and commercial services, and in the process grew into a global brand. "One of my biggest frustrations is that America really doesn't know everything we do. Our name and original service is so well known that people don't realize we're more than a drain cleaning company."

Rick wears his heart on his sleeve, whether talking about his wife and three daughters, or his goals in running Roto-Rooter. "My father hated his job at the factory, started drinking, and never stopped. It took a toll on our family. Then one day the factory just shut down, and men like my father were out of work without any chance of finding comparable jobs. One of my goals has been to ensure that the employees of Roto-Rooter never feel as ignored and ill treated as my father did." Rick believes it's vital to create an atmosphere in which people come to work and do their jobs well, not for the boss, but for themselves, because they take pride in what they do. "If we can't create a work environment where people want to come to work, and want to do their job all day long, then we're not getting it right."

> "There's never a better time than when things are tough to find out who you really are, as a person or as a company."

Because of this goal, Rick has tried to stay approachable and accessible. But he knows it's an uphill battle. "The title and trappings of the corner office are always barriers to totally honest communication. It's so easy to make a decision in a vacuum and then send out a company-wide e-mail or make some announcement in a corporate newsletter. Instead, you need to pause and find out how the decision impacts everyone."

Going undercover appealed to the operational side of Rick's personality, as it would give him a chance to see how the company's systems actually perform in the field. More important, it offered the motivational side of him an opportunity to at least temporarily bridge the barrier to honest communication and get a real sense of the problems and feelings of employees. That the country was in the midst of a great recession just added to Rick's desire to go undercover. "There's never a better time than when things are tough to find out who you really are, as a person or as a company." Rick was right about that, but in ways he never anticipated.

Rick decided to do as much of his undercover plumbing work as he could with one branch because it would minimize the number of managers with whom he'd have to break cover. For three assignments, he chose New Orleans because it was one of the company's fastest-growing operations despite covering a municipality that still hadn't recovered from the trauma of Hurricane Katrina. Keeping his plans a secret until he'd checked into his motel, Rick placed a call to Greg, the production supervisor. Putting Greg's mind at ease, the two conspirators plotted a week's worth of assignments for Hank Denman from the security of an empty motel courtyard. The operation wasn't beginning with much glamour, and it was only going to get messier.

JOB #1

Battling Blockages

Drain Tech, New Orleans LA

Rick, as eager as a Little Leaguer on the first day of practice, arrived for his assignment already dressed in his Roto-Rooter

uniform and sporting horned-rim glasses, Clark Kent–style, to help mask his identity. His trainer, Darrell, 52, would be taking him on a series of typical residential plumbing calls. Born and raised in New Orleans, Darrell explained to Rick that what he loved about his work was the chance to meet new people every day.

The first job was a tub that wouldn't drain. Rick crouched down in the few inches of dirty water that had failed to drain from the tub, and removed the drain lever with Darrell's guidance. The work was slow and unpleasant, and Darrell explained that tubs were always time-consuming calls. You never knew what might be causing the blockage. Rick first tried using an air pump to try to force the drain clear, but it was a messy failure, resulting in both his and Darrell's getting sprayed with dirty water. Rick then resorted to trying a long hook and then, when that failed, he had to overcome his disgust and go in with his naked fingers. He finally fished out an old washcloth that had somehow gotten into the drain. From the looks of the towel, it had been there for some time.

While driving between calls in the late afternoon, Darrell took a call from "the boss"—his wife. He sheepishly told Rick that his wife frequently checked on him because the previous spring he'd suffered chest pains that resulted in the discovery of a coronary blockage. Although the removal procedure was brief, the recovery took four months. Darrell was denied disability benefits and was forced to use up his savings to pay his bills. Something didn't sound right to Rick. "I knew he had health care coverage and benefits, so his situation didn't seem to make

 PRODUCERS' NOTE
What You Didn't See

It was evident the moment Rick first put on his Roto-Rooter blues that he was a man more comfortable working with his mind than with his hands. But at one point during Rick's undercover experience, he tried to force his mind to do too much. During one of the house calls Rick made with Darrell, it was necessary to remove the customer's toilet to clear out the drain. Darrell instructed Rick to start taking the weighty appliance off its base while he went outside to get something from the truck.

The whole time Darrell was gone, Rick didn't even make a move for his toolbox—he just stared at the toilet as if the bolts would magically unscrew themselves. When Darrell returned, he was duly unimpressed with Rick's attempt at telekinesis. The best advice Darrell, equal parts amused and annoyed, could give was to state the obvious: "Come on, Hank, that toilet's not gonna move all by itself!"

sense. I made a mental note to get in touch with the home office about the situation as soon as I got back to the motel."

Despite entreaties from "the boss," Darrell and Rick were still on the job at 8 P.M. Up on a roof, in the cold night air, Darrell showed Rick how to clean out a toilet line through the vent stack. After a few minutes of effort, a sulfurous odor came wafting out of the exhaust pipe, signaling that the clog was gone. "Smell that?" Darrell asked. "That's money."

Rick was struck by the inaccuracy of the company's time projections for the plumbing and drain cleaning repair jobs. "The job our system counted on being easy and quick, unclogging the tub, was more complex and took longer than estimated. And the jobs the system estimated being tougher and taking longer, like cleaning the system from the roof vent, took less time and were easier. We obviously have to rethink some of our models. It reinforced what plumbers had been telling me for years: that every job presents unique problems and challenges."

JOB #2

Color Me Red

Dispatcher, Call Center, Chicago, IL

Next, Rick headed north to Chicago to work an overnight shift as a dispatcher at the company's call center. He had a personal interest in this job because he'd been deeply involved in developing the dispatch system. He would get to take his own system for a test ride.

The manager of the call center assigned Rick to work with Candace, a stylish young woman whose outwardly friendly manner didn't disguise her annoyance at having to train a new hire.

Rick obsessively scribbled notes as Candace explained how the dispatch system functioned, with icons changing color depending on a technician's status. Finally, Rick copped to the problem he was having following her: he was color-blind. Acknowledging later the irony that someone who's color-blind developed a dispatch model based on color-coding, he explained, "I never intended to be doing it myself."

Candace and Rick took a break so that their increasing frustration with each other wouldn't bubble over. Over small talk, Candace revealed that she was a single mom with a three-year-old autistic son, who was being cared for by her parents because she couldn't afford day care. Rick was amazed at her ability to juggle so many things, but for Candace it was just a matter of keeping things in perspective. "If I can get caught up on my mortgage and I'm able to pay for day care, then things will be okay," she explained. "There are lots of people going through things like this every single day, so I don't complain."

Back at their work station, Rick was eager to handle a dispatch himself, despite Candace's sense that he wasn't quite ready yet. They compromised and had Rick speak with a customer while Candace listened and input the information. But Rick's telephone approach wasn't warm enough for Candace. She pointed out that Rick talked *at* the customers, rather than listening to them. "That makes the customer feel incompetent, helpless. I love my customers, and to convey that to them you need to be compassionate and understanding."

"There's a fine line you have to walk as a dispatcher," Rick conceded. "You need the customer to commit as quickly as possible, but you want them to feel good about the company and the process." Having the utmost admiration for Candace's perseverance and strength as a mom, he acknowledged their stylistic differences. "I think I'm at the sales end of the spectrum, and Candace is at the customer service end. She wanted to hold their hands, and I wanted to book the job and move on."

Rick admitted he'd come to the dispatch job thinking he'd be able to pick it up right away, and that it was an entirely technical task. "That was a reality check for me. We want people to be loyal to the Roto-Rooter brand, and to do that I'd need to have more of a customer service mentality. I'd need to be a lot warmer and fuzzier."

JOB #3

Jet Cleaning the Past

Sewer Maintenance, New Orleans LA

Warm and fuzzy weren't requirements for Rick's next undercover job: cleaning out clogged sewer pipes. The New Orleans branch was one of the first in the company to use high-pressure water-jet trucks to do sewer maintenance, and Rick hoped it was a service that could be brought to other markets.

The travel, discomfort, and pressure of being undercover were beginning to wear on Rick. But his spirits picked up when he met his trainer, 23-year-old Chris, who laughingly promised in a Louisiana drawl that Rick's hands would be dirty by the end of the day. On the way to their first call, Chris prepared Rick for what he was about to experience. "People flush things down the sewer line that don't belong there," he explained. "I used to like oatmeal. But I don't like oatmeal anymore because it reminds me of sewage."

Unable to rid that troubling analogy from his mind, Rick arrived at the job to find "oatmeal" backed up all over a parking lot, and a foul odor hanging in the air. Chris opened the cap to the sewer system, and raw sewage poured out. Getting more than just his hands dirty, Rick crouched amid the sewage

and pushed the hose nozzle into the pipe until it reached the clog. Chris then released a high-pressure blast of water that soon pushed the blockage clear, leaving Rick to hose the standing sewage off the parking lot and down the now open drain. Conceding that "Hank" might have a future with the company after his performance, Chris joked, "Who knows—he might be my boss one of these days."

With their work done, Chris and Rick chatted about how hard it can be to change and pick up new skills. Chris explained that he now embraced change and wasn't too proud to admit there was lots he could learn, and lots he wanted to learn. Chris revealed that he'd been in recovery for more than six years for addiction to alcohol and pills. "I realized I had a problem, and I had to go through rehab and change. Six-and-a-half years later I have no problems sharing it with anybody," Chris testified. "Today I have nothing to hide. Six-and-a-half years ago I had plenty to hide."

"I went into this undercover week thinking I'd probably get roughed up a bit on the jobs, but would come away learning a lot about the frontline employees and the company. The part I didn't anticipate was how much it would uncover me."

The admiration Rick felt for Chris's getting sober was obvious in his eyes as he listened to the young man's story. But there was far more going on with Rick than either man realized. Chris's frank confession coupled with Rick's physical and mental exhaustion just about brought the COO to his knees. "Things started racing through my head that I hadn't thought about since I was a kid," Rick recounted through tears. "My dad was an alcoholic, and it brought a lot of heartache to our family. Unfortunately, he went to his grave without he and I bringing closure to that issue. We never talked about our feelings, good or bad. I'm pretty sure he was proud of me and loved me, but you could have put a gun to his head and he still wouldn't have said it." An open, affectionate family man and an engaging, unpretentious boss, Rick had overcome his father's stoicism and alcoholism, yet those demons still clearly haunted him. "I don't know whether I was being naïve or simplistic, but I went into this undercover week thinking I'd probably get roughed up a bit on the jobs, but would come away learning a lot about the frontline employees and the company. The part I didn't anticipate was how much it would uncover me."

JOB #4

The Go-To Guy

Emergency Plumber, New Orleans LA

Rick had been told he couldn't leave New Orleans without working with Henry, the technician who was routinely assigned the trickiest jobs. A trim man with a closely cut mustache and a military bearing, Henry is experienced in some of the unique problems facing plumbers in a city with very old housing stock that is actually below sea level. As a result, Henry has become a source of expertise and advice for most of the other technicians in the area. After a polite but short greeting, the go-to guy let

Rick know they had to get on the road because there was a customer waiting.

Arriving at their call, Henry and Rick met an elderly woman who said sewage was backing up under her house. Henry sent Rick under the house with a flashlight looking for the sewage pipe. Moving slowly like an infantryman under fire, Rick inched his way under the structure, crawling through the sewage, heeding Henry's warning to watch out for rats. "If I see a rat under here, I'll be screaming like a little girl," Rick warned. Rick found the sewer opening, and Henry, using a cable-mounted camera system, was able to spot the problem: a break in the pipe under the lawn. Henry explained to the homeowner that it was a major repair job, with a price tag of $1,200. Distressed and on the verge of tears, the homeowner lamented that her medical bills meant she couldn't afford the service. In an aside, Henry told Rick that when he meets good people under financial duress, he feels compelled to do all he can to help. Henry went back to the woman and asked her if she could afford $500. She said she could, and Henry promised he'd have someone there the next day.

"We give our technicians discretion to price as needed, so we try not to have hard-and-fast rules, but I was still taken aback by Henry giving such an extreme discount," Rick admitted. "Then I remembered that Henry works on commission. He was taking money out of his *own* pocket. He was getting her house up and running again, putting his heart and his wallet out there for her."

After a day of tough jobs and phone interruptions from other plumbers needing Henry's advice, Rick went with Henry to watch him coach his son's basketball team, which he did four nights a week. Pulling up to the gym in their Roto-Rooter van, Henry and Rick were met by Henry's wife, Pat, who'd been shuttling some of the kids back and forth in the family's pickup to make sure they got to practice and wouldn't be hanging out on the streets.

Watching Henry with his family triggered feelings of loneliness in the already vulnerable Rick. On the phone with his wife later that evening, he recounted working with Henry and watching him coach his son, and all the emotion he felt after his conversation with Chris, reexposing the still fresh wound. "I feel like I was cheated out of having a relationship, not just with my father but with my mother and sister as well. We figured out that the way to survive in that house was to keep our emotions bottled up inside. My older sister is ill, and it wasn't until two weeks ago that we actually said we loved each other. I don't like everything that my father did, but I've finally figured out that it's okay to forgive him and move on." There was one more stop on that path, however.

JOB #5

JA Spark Ignites

Welder, Roto-Rooter Manufacturing Plant, Des Moines IA

Rick's last day undercover brought him back to where it all started for Roto-Rooter in 1935, the Des Moines plant that manufactures the machines the company's technicians use to clear out drains. Besides its being a homecoming for the president and COO of Roto-Rooter, it was also a homecoming of sorts for Rick Arquilla the man, who had been thinking a great deal about his factory worker father.

Rick's trainer for the day, Dan, a stocky, ever smiling presence on the shop floor, was unmissable due to the shower of sparks cascading from his welding station. Putting on an American flag–design headscarf, a protective coat, and a welder's mask, Rick tried his hand at the job. From the start there was a problem: he was having a hard time seeing through the welding mask. "I tried it with my glasses on and with my glasses off. I tried getting closer and tried going further away. My being color-blind didn't help, either."

Patient coaching by Dan, who's unable to wear his own glasses under the welding mask, did nothing to ease Rick's frustrations. When Rick sent a spark flying into his shoe, burning his foot, the two men agreed it was time for a break. "I don't need you to train me how to take a break," Rick laughed. "That's one thing I can do right." But despite the outward display of humor, Rick was annoyed at himself. "I really thought welding would be a nice reprieve from all the drain and sewer cleaning. I thought I'd hit it out of the park. Actually it was probably the hardest task I'd faced, and I was forced to eat a little more humble pie."

Over a cup of coffee to help wash down that humble pie, Rick and Dan talked about the latter's love of muscle cars and how he and a number of the other workers got together in their free time to work on them. The conversation took a serious turn when Dan explained how work at the factory was the slowest he'd seen in his thirteen years with the company. That, coupled with the closing of so many other local factories, had the staff on edge. "A lot of us are worried the company's going to shut down the plant or move it overseas to manufacture things there. We got some people here that are getting close to retiring, and they're concerned." There was real pain on Rick's face as he listened. When Dan suggested they head back to the shop floor, Rick begged off, saying he'd slowed Dan down enough.

But it wasn't his concern about slowing Dan down or suffering another self-inflicted hot foot that led Rick to step aside; he needed to gather his emotions. Rick had begun his undercover journey hoping that his employees didn't feel as ignored and ill-treated as his father had. "I don't know if my dad were working here today that he'd say this is a great place to work."

PRODUCERS' NOTE
What You Didn't See

After meeting Dan and learning about the sorry state of morale at his production plant, Rick couldn't bring himself to wait until the finale to reveal his true identity and start making changes within the company. When he chose not to return to Dan's welding station following his break, Rick didn't sulk or wallow in his self-pity—he got himself fired up and marched directly into the on-site manager's office.

The manager was confused at first about why the new recruit from the 75th-anniversary documentary had so much to say about the state of the plant. But all doubt vanished when Rick broke character and explained who he was and what he wanted to do about the situation. Vowing to take responsibility for the problems rather than point fingers and assign blame, Rick immediately sat down with the manager and began brainstorming ways to improve working conditions right on the spot.

Tears coming to his eyes, Rick spoke about what he'd felt, not just because of that short time on the shop floor, but after his week of working with his frontline employees. "These workers get up every day, and they work this hard because that's what they're supposed to do; it's their job. I give a damn about the people who go out there and bust their asses. If it sucks for them to show up every day, that's on me," he insisted, his voice breaking with emotion. "Yes, we have a business to run, and we need to make money. And yes, I need to perform at a high enough level to get my ticket punched so I can come back and work again next year. But someday people are going to stand over my coffin, and what are they going to say? 'Here lies old Rick. He made a lot of money for Roto-Rooter.' Well, what else? If that's all they can say, then I would really have let this company down. I should be able to do a lot more."

HE REVEALS THE TRUTH

The trip from Des Moines to Cincinnati gave Rick little time to recover from what had been a physically and emotionally draining undercover week. Even though Rick was running on fumes, he got right to work dealing with what he'd learned while undercover. He reported on his experiences to his executive committee, and got the ball rolling on some ideas he'd developed, such as offering access to health counseling and financial planning services. Then it was time for him to reveal his true identity to each of his bosses from the week, after bringing them to headquarters for a series of surprise meetings.

When Rick told Darrell, his first boss in New Orleans, that he wasn't "Hank," Darrell jokingly asked if he was Hank's brother. Rick had been concerned that Darrell had paid all of his medical bills out of pocket, when he was a fully insured employee. Once back at headquarters, Rick had the home office investigate Darrell's disability claim, and they'd discovered there had been a mistake in the paperwork. The insurance company would be making good on all the money Darrell had unnecessarily spent out of pocket. Rick stressed that the company wanted Darrell to be out in the field meeting new people and turning them into loyal customers for years to come. To make sure of that, the company would be putting a home gym in his house, sending him to a nutritionist, and setting up an account for him at a local health food shop. "I get the feeling that it's not just that he's president of the company," Darrell said after. "It's a personal thing for him to get involved."

Dan recognized his failed welding trainee instantly and smiled broadly when Rick walked in. After revealing his true identity, Rick expressed his admiration for Dan's work ethic. Dan reiterated that he loved his job, but that he was worried that "someday I might pull in the parking lot and that there would be a big sign on the door saying 'Closed.'" Rick asked Dan to tell everyone at the factory that Roto-Rooter would not be outsourcing its manufacturing and would be staying right there in Des Moines. And to help boost morale, Rick said the company would be setting up a garage at which Dan and the other shop employees could work on their cars. Rick also promised to personally visit the Des Moines plant more often than he had in the past.

Candace was speechless when she learned the true identity of the guy who'd had such a hard time grasping the dispatch system, admitting she had been furious with him. Rick explained how much he admired how, without complaint, she dealt with all that had been thrown her way. He told her the company would pay the cost of her enrolling her son in an autism program, and give her $5,000 to apply toward her mortgage. "I'm going to be able to do a lot more for my son. I'm so happy and overwhelmed. It's incredible."

Henry, the go-to man on whom every other plumber relied for advice, couldn't believe his trainee was president of the company. Rick explained that he was impressed not just by Henry's skill on the job but by how much he gave of himself. "You're the most selfless person I know," Rick told him. "I'm not happy how you and your wife have to go back and forth picking those kids up for practice, so the company is going to give you a 15-person van so you can transport the whole team." Receiving the keys, Henry shook his head in disbelief and gratitude. But then Rick continued. "We're going to move you into management, making you a field supervisor, and we're going to give you a raise." "When you work hard and do the right thing, it pays off," said a choked-up Henry.

Chris, the recovering addict with an aversion to oatmeal, did a double take when he saw Rick enter the office. It was cathartic for Rick to finally reveal to Chris what their conversations had meant to him and why. Discussing his father's alcoholism, its effect on the family, and how they'd never reconciled, once again brought tears to Rick's eyes. Rick expressed his admiration for Chris's strength—"I wish my Dad had done what you're doing"—and asked if Chris would be willing to travel around to different cities and speak about alcoholism and addiction to Roto-Rooter employees. Chris, visibly moved, accepted immediately, saying that if he could help one person, then it would make what he'd been through worthwhile.

Having reconnected with all his coworkers from the past week, Rick went down to address the headquarters staff who had gathered, they thought, for another of the ongoing 75th-anniversary celebrations. Rick instead revealed he'd been working undercover for the past week and showed clips of his experiences. Joking with the crowd gave Rick a few minutes' respite from the emotional roller coaster he'd been riding for almost two weeks. As soon as he turned serious, however, the tears that had been emerging on and off for much of his undercover experience flowed again. Momentarily turning his back on the crowd to gather himself once more, Rick turned back and offered a special thanks to the people with whom he'd worked undercover. "To each and every one of you, thanks. You taught me not just how to do the work but also how to be a better person. And for that I'm grateful."

After the hugs and tears were finished, Rick was able to reflect further. "I can't remember a stretch of time, personally or professionally, that was more difficult yet more gratifying than this. I learned some things about the company that I didn't know, and I learned some things about people that I didn't know. Probably most difficult and gut wrenching of all was something I learned about myself. I always said, someday I'll get around to finding closure with my father; someday I'll get around to telling my sister I love her. But I'm too busy right now. I'm an important executive who has a business to run, so I can't find ways to squeeze all that in too. Well, you know what, all the people I met, they have burdens, and they work incredibly hard, yet they've found the time to deal with their demons. So I'm pretty sure I can too."

SINCE THE SHOW

★ **Darrell** received the check for the disability funds he was due and is now working out regularly on his home gym. Roto-Rooter also arranged for him to enroll in a physical therapy program, which he attends three times a week, first thing in the morning so he's not too tired after a full day's work.

★ **Chris** is taking public speaking training in preparation for going out to speak to others about alcoholism and addiction.

★ **Dan** was thrilled to return to the factory in Des Moines and reassure his coworkers that their jobs would not be outsourced. To demonstrate Roto-Rooter's commitment to the plant, a new air-conditioning system has been installed. Rick has also arranged for Dan and his colleagues to have access to a garage and equipment to work on their muscle cars.

★ **Candace** applied the $5,000 to her mortgage, making her finances more manageable, and enrolled her son in the leading autism program in Chicago.

★ **Henry's** team used their team van well. It took them to a national championship tournament.

★ **Rick** is still president and chief operating officer of Roto-Rooter. He and his management team have worked hard to keep up the positive momentum generated by Rick's *Undercover Boss* experience. "We started thinking about all the people who weren't on the show," Rick explained. "It was great that five people made the show and were helped, but we wanted to make sure we launched company-wide initiatives that helped everyone. We've started programs to help people get ahead in their careers, take care of their health, and better manage their personal finances. It was clear to us that we should use *Undercover Boss* as a springboard to do a lot of ongoing good for a lot of people, and not just leave it as one fleeting moment of euphoria for a handful of people."

The experience also had an obvious personal impact on Rick. He has no regrets about being the most tear-stricken undercover boss of the first season. "Being on the show was like riding an emotional roller coaster, and sharing it with the viewing audience. The experiences were coming hard and fast, and I was trying to process them all while staying in the role of Hank Denman. There was a point when I just said, 'I'm not holding back. They're going to see all and know all.' I believe that if you're willing to put yourself out there

"It was clear to us that we should use Undercover Boss *as a springboard to do a lot of ongoing good for a lot of people, and not just leave it as one fleeting moment of euphoria for a handful of people."*

and take the journey, there's a good chance you'll end up in a better place. I have. It's hard to believe that I could bring closure to the issue of my father's battle with alcoholism via a national television show, but that's what really happened," he insisted. "A door that I had closed as a young adult, and had kept closed for 40 years, was opened, and I took those issues head-on, thought them through, and have moved on. I'm not harboring any anger, and I'm certainly not keeping anything a secret. After all, a few million people know about it now."

SAY IT WITH FLOWERS

"We're Irish Catholic brothers from New York City, He's the oldest and I'm the youngest. This is the only way we know how to treat each other."

Chris McCann
COO, 1-800-Flowers.com

Patrick O'Reilly
Unemployed Housepainter

How We Found the Boss

Family-owned and operated businesses are increasingly hard to find these days. Family businesses that have grown into multimillion dollar corporations are even more rare. When one such business is run by an executive team consisting of two brothers—the oldest and youngest of five siblings—we knew that company would make an unusual episode of Undercover Boss. We had originally conceived 1-800-Flowers as somewhat of a tag-team episode, highlighting how the power of teamwork and brotherly love can make a successful business. But in addition to being the founder, older brother Jim McCann was also the face of the company appearing in 1-800-Flowers television commercials since the 1990s. Since Jim was far too recognizable to actually go undercover, his little brother—president and COO Chris McCann—was ready and willing to step up and handle the assignment.

THE BOSS

Chris McCann, president and COO.

HIS COVER

Patrick O'Reilly, an out-of-work house painter who's been enlisted by a television crew making a documentary about entry-level jobs.

HIS COMPANY

If you've sent flowers or candy recently, you're probably one of the millions worldwide who have shopped at 1-800-Flowers .com, the leading florist and gift shop in the world, with annual revenues of nearly $700 million. Founded in 1976 as a single retail store in Manhattan, the company has since grown into a gifting powerhouse with a leading e-commerce brand and more than 150 franchised and company-owned retail stores and more than 7,000 florist shop affiliates. Although the company's heart and soul is its floral business, it has acquired and launched other brands and companies to expand its gift offerings, such as Fannie May, the iconic chocolate producer; Cheryl's, maker of fresh-baked cookies, brownies, and cakes; The Popcorn Factory, which offers gourmet popcorn and other snacks in designer tins; and even WineTasting.com. Its goal is to offer all the products their customers need to send smiles to the important people in his or her life.

HIS STORY

It's not easy being a little brother. Sure, you've got a protector and confidant in your big brother, someone you've undoubtedly looked up to from a young age. But you've also got a lifelong rival and tease; someone accustomed to being bigger and stronger, and seeing you as the little one. And more often than not, someone who knows exactly how to push your buttons, and can't resist doing so.

Chris McCann was determined to shed his little-brother status once and for all. As president and COO of 1-800-Flowers

.com, he's responsible for the overall performance, direction, and organization of one of the most successful multichannel retailers in the United States. You'd think that having managed his organization's transition from retail floral chain to international teleflorist to the most popular Internet gift shop, Chris wouldn't take a backseat to anyone. However, his big brother Jim, the company's congenial founder and CEO, is very comfortable behind the wheel. And like every big brother, Jim wasn't going to move to the passenger seat without a loving shove.

Raised in a blue-collar neighborhood, the five McCann siblings learned about business and working together as a family from their parents.

"When we first got into the telephone ordering business, we set up the operation in our Bayside, Queens, store. We stripped out the middle of the store, and Jim and I built 30 telemarketing stations out of plywood. The front of the store was for retail, the back for design, and the phones were in the middle. People would come in and ask us if we were running a bookmaking operation. We'd joke and tell them no, the margins would be much better if we were bookies."

McCann Painting and Decorating was started by their grandparents, and run out of the family home. Jim is the oldest, followed by Julie, Kevin, Peggy, and then the baby, Chris. Kevin, who's developmentally disabled, was and remains the nucleus of the family around whom they all rally.

In 1976, Jim borrowed $10,000 from family and friends to buy a small flower shop called Flora Plenty on Manhattan's Upper East Side. He intended for the profits from the shop to supplement the modest income he earned as a social worker. And just as they had with the family business, Jim's younger siblings came to help out their big brother in his new flower shop. Chris started working there part-time when he was 15.

"There's a famous saying about it being lonely at the top. Jim and I have spoken about how fortunate we are that we have each other to talk to, bounce ideas off, and to joke with."

Before long, the business had grown into a chain of local flower shops, and in 1984, Jim asked Chris to join him in the florist business instead. "We sat down in an Irish pub, and Jim said he thought we had an opportunity to build something big, and that he could really use someone to run the stores and operations," Chris recalled. Though he had been planning to go to law school, Chris agreed to set that ambition aside and throw in his lot with his brother in a bid to build an enduring business. "We agreed on a six-month contract. I think I'm now on my 68th six-month contract."

Over the course of the next 25 years the company expanded steadily. Through the acquisition of the 1-800-Flowers telephone number they moved into telephone sales, then spread franchised retail outlets across the country, developed online sales though their Web site and formed strategic partnerships, and made acquisitions of other gift-related businesses. Despite its growth, 1-800-Flowers.com is still very much a family business: besides Jim and Chris, sister Julie works as one of the firm's lead designers, and brother Kevin works in the company's greenhouse affiliates. And there are still the equal parts loving and teasing, support and competitive battles waged by big brother and little brother. Chris noted, "There's a famous saying about it being lonely at the top. Jim and I have spoken about how fortunate we are that we have each other to talk to, bounce ideas off, and to joke with."

And they fully know how they complement each other's strengths: Chris calls Jim a visionary and a marketing genius, and Jim calls Chris a brilliant organizer and the ultimate pragmatist. Despite their clear success, the brothers share one regret. "Both our parents died at early ages," Chris revealed. "Jim and I often sit and talk about how we wish they got to see the success we've had. They would have been proud of us." Because of the early deaths of their parents and the difference in his and Chris's ages, Jim has at times played the protective, domineering older brother. Old habits die hard.

Although the two men rarely pass up an opportunity to needle each other, they share an obvious affection as well. They are determined never to hold a grudge, inspired in part by their late father's alienation from his own brother due to a business disagreement. "We've never had an argument that lasts beyond the

"For all the years we've been working together, Jim still sees me as his little brother."

argument," Chris explained. And whenever outsiders take exception to Jim's teasing, Chris rises to his brother's defense. "We're Irish Catholic brothers from New York City," he stated, as if that said it all. "He's the oldest and I'm the youngest. This is the only way we know how to treat each other."

Because Jim's face is too well known as the face of the company from their television and print ads, the brothers decided that Chris would be the one to go undercover, working at entry-level jobs inside their company for a week. With the assumption that Chris will gradually take on more and more of Jim's role as leader of the company, the younger brother was also eager to make it clear that he's ready, willing, and able to assume the mantle. "For all the years we've been working together, Jim still

PRODUCERS' NOTE
What You Didn't See

Chris took his undercover mission very seriously, even before he was in the field. Prior to participating in the show, most bosses keep their families in the loop—confidentially, of course—in addition to having a meeting with their executive staff about the process and the goals of the experience. But Chris played everything very close to the vest and, though he did tell his wife, he didn't divulge anything to his kids.

When asked why he was growing a beard, Chris merely said that he was trying out a new look. And what about his approaching 10-day absence? Just another routine business trip. What makes Chris's secrecy more strange: his kids watched *Undercover Boss* regularly and were big fans!

sees me as his little brother," Chris admitted. "But I'm his partner in this business; sometimes I need to remind him of that." So while his outward motivation for Chris's going undercover was to get him back in touch with the front line, there was also a more personal motive for Chris as well: proving to his big brother that he has what it takes to be the boss.

Even on the day before Chris began his undercover adventure, the two brothers couldn't resist falling into their usual banter: Jim threatened to spy on Chris, and Chris parried that he was used to his brother's interference, so it wouldn't be anything new. As it turned out, he shouldn't have spoken so fast.

JOB #1

Designing Doldrums

1-800-Flowers Store, South Plainfield NJ

Fully committed to his alias, Paddy, an out-of-work housepainter, Chris grew a beard (which, ironically, made him look even more like Jim) and donned eyeglasses. His first undercover job: working with a store's floral designer. It turned out to be something of a mixed blessing. He was eager to experience a job that played a central role in the company's success. "We need to make sure that the designers' creativity really comes through, because without their skills, we don't have anything to sell." But at the same time, he knew from past experience that he was no artist. Pauline, his coworker for the day, would come to agree.

Pauline has spent the majority of her 32 years around flowers. As a little girl she'd tag along with her father, who sold flowers out of the back of his car. When she was a teenager and her father became a flower wholesaler, Pauline started doing floral designs in her parents' basement.

It's that background and experience that helped Pauline come up with her own original designs to meet customers' unique requests. "I've made everything from teddy bears to cheeseburgers out of flowers," she told Chris. Going over the company's current catalog of standard designs with her trainee, Pauline explained that she'd love to bring some of her own creativity to the collection, but the designs were put together by "someone in corporate."

Initially annoyed at having to train someone while getting her own work done, Pauline quickly warmed to the task because of how hard Chris was trying. In an effort to inspire Chris's creative side, she urged him to "have fun with it" as they worked on arrangements side by side to meet the day's orders. Chris's inner artist, however, remained deeply buried. He thought he might be improving as they worked their way through 20 arrangements, but Pauline was frank. "You're trying hard," she acknowledged, "but I don't think you'd last in this business."

> "It's not enough for us to just have a relationship with the franchise owner and tell them about our programs," he realized. "We need to have a relationship with every employee working for our brand."

As they grew to know each other over the course of the day, Pauline shared some of her professional frustrations with Chris, in response to his questions about her happiness at the company overall. Describing how boring it became making the same designs over and over again, and pointing out that some of the long-standing designs hadn't changed for years, Pauline offered that the company needed to "step it up a notch." She told Chris that she regularly attends flower shows on her own time (and at her owns expense), and that she sees new trends are emerging in the marketplace turning floral design into more of an art.

A bit stung by Pauline's candid criticism of the older designs, Chris was even more upset when he learned that she paid to attend the flower shows out of her own pocket and that she received no ongoing training. "I've talked to people in corporate and asked them why there's no ongoing training, but I've never gotten a real answer," Pauline explained. Chris shook his head in sympathy, but inside he was steaming. But he couldn't break cover, no matter how great the temptation.

"We provide ongoing training," he insisted later, his frustration matching Pauline's. "We have design councils she could be a part of to provide input into the product line. We've got the programs she wants; she just doesn't know about them."

Chris recognized that Pauline's frustration stemmed from a lack of communication with retail shops. "It's not enough for us to just have a relationship with the franchise owner and tell them about our programs," he realized. "We need to have a relationship with every employee working for our brand."

JOB #2

Bittersweet Discoveries

Fannie May Factory, Canton OH

Although Chris's hands-on knowledge of chocolate was limited to eating it, he had some concrete goals in mind for the day he'd spend on the line at the company's Fannie May factory. "Right now, the plant produces about 10 million pounds of chocolate per year. I need to make sure we can ramp that up to anywhere between 16 and 20 million pounds per year to meet the kind of demand we project our online operations will generate."

One of the people he'd be relying on to meet these new production goals was Nicole, an earthy brunette who'd be his trainer for his day undercover. Despite having worked at the plant for only four years, the 36-year-old was responsible for supervising the operation of one of the more important pieces

of equipment in the factory: the enrober. The giant machine takes anywhere from 7,000 to 11,000 pounds of pretzels an hour and covers them in chocolate, sending them down conveyer belts to be bulk-wrapped and packaged for shipment in 30-pound cartons.

With visions of the classic *I Love Lucy* episode running through his head, Chris was stationed at one of the "bulking" positions, where he'd be responsible for assembling and positioning cartons to catch the finished chocolates as they fell off the belt. Chris did his best to bounce between the box station and the belts of streaming product, but he barely managed to keep up. After a short while, chocolate covered pretzels were scattered across the floor at his station. Chris's frenetic efforts were offset by Nicole's calm, efficient assistance. Whenever the pace threatened to become overwhelming she would step in and handily set things right and then depart again leaving Chris to struggle.

"It's vital that you also connect with your people. . . . That's the way Jim built our company: by listening to the workers."

As the shift wore on, Chris found the best he could do was to apologize for failing to keep up. He asked Nicole about the factory's productivity goals and who set them. She explained that the target at this station was 1,100 pounds an hour, and confessed that she had no idea how management had come up with the figure, seeing as how "the people who set the goals never come out to see how hard we have to work." Chris was stunned. The managers of the chocolate factory were some of the top operational executives in the company, and the plant appeared to be one of the company's best run business units. And yet he had just experienced firsthand an exceptionally tough productivity mandate set by absentee management.

As the day wore on, Chris developed a rhythm for the job, and the piles of chocolate-covered pretzels littering his work station shrunk. By the end of their shift, Nicole actually high-fived him for exceeding the goal. But when Chris expectantly asked whether there were incentives or bonuses in place for beating targets or exceeding their goals, Nicole told him that none existed.

Reflecting on his debut as a chocolatier, Chris pointed out that "this was a great lesson illustrating that no matter how productive you are as a manager and a leader, it's vital that you also connect with your people. We should be doing that. That's the way Jim built our company: by listening to the workers. That's how we learn. I can't help wondering how much more productive we could be if we listened to people like Nicole and engaged them in the process. There are all sorts of different studies on why employees stay or leave a company. Compensation is never at the top of the list. It's always whether or not they feel connected. Two ways to foster that are to recognize their contributions and to ask for their input."

JOB #3

Forming Real, Rather Than Virtual, Relationships

1-800-Flowers Store, Boston

Over the past few years much of the company's efforts have been directed toward expanding their Internet operations.

Chris wondered whether this might have come at the expense of the retail side of the business. So he scheduled an undercover mission at one of the company's top-grossing shops, located in Boston's historic North End, a tightly knit, middle-class, urban neighborhood.

Dee, the store's manager-florist, put Chris to work immediately, having him cut flowers for bouquets that she was assembling. Exuding stylish warmth, Dee told Chris she had been with the company for two years, but had more than 20 years' experience as a retail florist. And that experience showed in Dee's masterful customer service. As customers arrived at the cozy store throughout the day, they were greeted like old friends. People came in not just to buy flowers but also to see Dee and chat. "These people are coming to my home," Dee said proudly, "so I want them to feel at home."

At one point, Dee introduced Chris to a four-year-old who'd accompanied his mother into the shop. Calling him "her boyfriend," she helped the little boy pick out a flower of his own. Chris was beaming with a joy that matched the toddler's. Memories of the McCann's first flower shop flooded back to him. "I thought back to all our regulars: Ellen; Big Paulie, the neighborhood bookie; and Phyllis, who, in my 15-year-old impressionable eyes, was the most beautiful woman in the world."

Chris's reverie was shattered when Steve, the store's general manager, arrived to help make the day's deliveries. Realizing he'd met Steve before, Chris worried that his cover might be blown. With all the subtlety and effectiveness of Austin Powers, Chris banished himself to the corner, where he wiped down the glass cooler doors with intense focus, refusing to look up, let alone make eye contact. Luckily Steve had neither recognized nor noticed Chris. Disaster had been averted—but only for a moment.

Suddenly Dee called Chris over and asked him to help Steve deliver some arrangements to a restaurant up the street.

"Customers don't have a relationship with a company; they have a relationship with the people who work for that company."

At first Chris tried to hide his face behind the tall arrangement he was carrying. But figuring he would soon be recognized, Chris seized the opportunity of being out of the shop and on the street to reveal his identity to the general manager. Peering around the flowers, he asked, "Hey, Steve, do you recognize me?" The general manager craned his head around the tall arrangement he was carrying. "Chris? Holy shit!" Chris made Steve promise to keep his secret, barely managing to save his undercover mission.

As he finished out his shift, Chris marveled that Dee had the type of spirit they hoped to foster throughout the company, at all levels. "Customers don't have a relationship with a company; they have a relationship with the people who work for that company," he explained. "Dee is a living example of what my brother always says: build a relationship first, do business second. I've always admired Jim's ability to understand and connect with people quickly. That's something I've got to work on if I'm going to be their leader."

JOB #4

A Tale of Two Cities

1-800-Flowers Store, Waban MA

Determined to make sure that his undercover retail experience covered the range of company stores, Chris next went to work at a newer retail shop in Waban, an affluent suburban village west of Boston.

Like Dee from the North End store, Sheryl, the manager-florist of the Waban store, was a recent recruit to 1-800-Flowers who had two decades of floral experience. A hardworking, alabaster blonde, Sheryl had owned her own store for 14 years.

At the beginning of his shift, Chris was assigned to process new flower deliveries while Sheryl worked preparing arrangements at the other end of the spacious store. It was several hours before the first walk in customer of the day arrived. Reacting to the empty sales floor she asked if the store had just opened.

Sheryl explained that it had actually been open for over a year. Chris could see the shop was facing problems immediately.

Sure enough, that serendipitous customer was one of the few to visit the store that day. Unable to conceal his concern, Chris asked Sheryl about the typical traffic patterns in the store and confirmed his worst fears: woefully scant walk-ins. Acknowledging that the lack of local customers was unlike anything she'd experienced in her previous shops, a frustrated Sheryl attributed the problem to the store's name. "This is a very ritzy neighborhood with lots of old money. I've had customers tell me that they like my arrangements, but won't buy anything for friends because they don't want them to see our name on it." Chris was aghast.

Sheryl went on to say she knew that community outreach was needed to make the neighbors aware that the shop was a

PRODUCERS' NOTE
What You Didn't See

Sheryl is definitely a cheerleader for the 1-800-Flowers brand, with a real knack for spreading the word through outreach and promotion. But her experience with cheerleading goes beyond her role in the flower shop: Sheryl owns a company that teaches girls (including her two daughters, both former cheerleaders) how to cheer and dance. The company is engaged in continual fundraising so that it can provide its services without charging its students tuition or fees. After meeting Sheryl during *Undercover Boss,* Chris McCann was happy to make a donation himself.

high-quality, full-service, retail florist, not just a call center as the 1-800 name suggested to some. Unfortunately, she was tethered to the store and unable to visit local catering halls, dance studios, and schools to spread the word. It didn't help that the shop hadn't done any local advertising or promotion.

Upset but not surprised by Sheryl's comment, Chris admitted that the company's name was something of a Catch-22: "The brand is so strong, but it can also be confusing on a storefront sign. We've done a great job over the years of translating the brand from a telephone business to an Internet business. Now we have to do just as good a job translating it back into a retail business." Admitting that the company's marketing had been focused on driving customers online, Chris felt guilty about letting Sheryl down. "I've been in Sheryl's position," he acknowledged. "Jim used to send me out to the new stores to get them up and running. Jim and I grew up as florists. We *still* think of ourselves as florists. Sheryl and the other retailers need more of our support."

JOB #5

Back to the Future

1-800-Flowers Store, Brooklyn

On his final day undercover, Chris went in search of his future. "I'm looking toward the next 10-year wave of growth for our business," said the leader-in-waiting. "Our stores are going to be the focus of that effort; I want to see what kind of young people are coming into the business." Ironically, Chris's goal of precognition stirred up a hornet's nest of nostalgia.

PRODUCERS' NOTE
What You Didn't See

Our crew was as instantly taken with Jose as our viewers were. What you didn't see: beneath Jose's smiling demeanor and impressive work ethic lies the heart of a warrior. In addition to his talents for arranging flowers and motivating his staff, Jose is also an accomplished practitioner of mixed martial arts. Every day after he leaves the shop, he attends practice to hone his skills. The discipline he has gained through his training has prepared him well for his management position, and has provided him with the focus and energy necessary to excel.

Told that the company's shop in Bay Ridge, Brooklyn, had the company's youngest dispatcher–production manager, Chris returned to his New York City roots for a visit. Chris found Jose, a lanky 19-year-old with a chinstrap beard, supervising a team of 12, who were cutting, designing, wrapping, and delivering arrangements. He was also managing the well-stocked retail shop. As Chris worked around the store, arranging merchandise, he couldn't help but be struck by Jose. Earnest and enthusiastic, Jose had been working since he was a teenager, when the premature death of his father forced him to get a part-time job to contribute to his family's support. Chris was incredibly impressed by the young manager.

Inspired by Jose's work ethic and personal story, which more than a little mirrored his own, Chris embraced his job as Jose's general helper. At first, Jose was a bit concerned that Chris was "a little overmature" for the job. But soon he found the trainee surprisingly eager to please and hardworking. Clearing trimmings off the floor in the work area, sweeping around the feet of the designers, and hustling to restock the flowers the designers needed for their arrangements, Chris fitted in perfectly on Jose's efficient team. But then, one of his coworkers took a closer look at him. "You look familiar; you ever work at the Bethpage store?" the curious employee asked. Despite Chris's panicked tone, the inquisitive designer accepted his denial. Chris's nerves were on edge.

His nerves were strained even further when Jose announced he'd received a call from the company headquarters announcing that CEO Jim McCann was in the area and wanted to stop by. Jose and the staff hustled around the shop like courtiers trying to make things perfect for a royal visit. Chris, in contrast, was thinking of ways to kill the king. After the fiasco with Steve up in Boston, and the curiosity of his coworker, Chris worried that the surprise visit would be the straw that broke the camel's back in his attempt to keep his identity a secret. What's worse, Jim hadn't bothered to check with Chris before pulling the stunt. "He could have called me. I understand him wanting to check on how it's going, but he could have waited until later. I wish he'd just let me do my job," he groused.

With the store ready for a white-glove inspection, Jim made his entrance. Warm and gregarious as ever, Jim quickly charmed the young women working the front of the shop and set Jose at ease. As he toured the shop, Jim had a good word for just about everyone—except, of course, the new trainee. As Jim quizzed Jose about the rookie's performance (all in front of "Paddy"), it was hard to tell which was more likely to blow Chris's cover— Jim's obvious joy in teasing him, or Chris's increasingly frayed nerves. Finally, after offering some criticisms of Chris's technique as he prepared an arrangement under his brother's judgmental eye, Jim decided he'd tortured his youngest brother enough, and made a triumphant exit.

The McCann brothers had previously arranged to meet at an area diner after Chris's shift ended, to discuss his week undercover. Chris was still annoyed with the surprise visit when he arrived, but as soon as the two brothers made eye contact, they both burst into laughter, and all was forgiven. Relating how much he enjoyed the undercover experience, Chris recounted stories of those he'd met. "I was with a lady up in the North End of Boston, and moms and kids were coming to give her presents. It was . . ."

". . . like our shop on First Avenue," Jim said, finishing the thought. "Brings back memories . . ."

". . . of the way it started," Chris agreed. He turned serious. "I also learned there are some things I need to change. I know I'm your little brother, but I need you to trust me. After all, I'm running the company."

HE REVEALS THE TRUTH

Chris began instituting changes as soon as he arrived back at the company's Carle Place headquarters. His coworkers from his undercover experience had all been brought to Long Island, still unaware of the identity of their trainee.

Nicole looked nervous when she found out Chris's true identity, but his smile put her at ease. Keenly aware of how hard Nicole worked, Chris promised that she would be part of the process of setting production goals from now on. "Not only that, but your hard work and great attitude inspired me to create an incentive program so you can make more money when you exceed your goals." Nicole was grateful, not just for the promise of input and bonuses but also for someone noticing how hard she worked.

Excited to be at headquarters after working for the company for so long, Pauline was shocked when her former trainee entered the office. After revealing his true identity, Chris reminded her that she'd told him how her dream was to have some input into the company's designs. "I'm going to make that dream come true." He explained that he was going to arrange for her to spend time training with the design council, and that she'd work with them to come up with one of the company's next collections. With tears rolling down her cheeks, Pauline said the opportunity meant the world to her. "My dad has been gone for eight years. He's the one who encouraged me to get to where I am today. I know he's looking down on me proudly."

Dee looked as though she'd seen a ghost when Chris entered the office. Breaking his cover, Chris said he'd come up to Boston to work at her store because it was one of the highest grossing in the company, and he wanted to find out why. "I learned the secret," he said. "The secret is you." Saying he'd come up with a way to honor her incredible customer service skills, Chris told Dee that although the company had never named one of its arrangements after a person, that was about to change. Dee's lips quivered and her eyes began to water as she buried her face in her hands, understanding what was about to come next. "Your customers step into a little bit of paradise when they come to your shop, so I'd like to call the arrangement Dee's Paradise."

When Sheryl saw her former trainee enter, she rose confidently to shake his hand. Chris got right to the point, asking if she remembered telling him about the biggest challenge she faced. "Of course. I told you that the public thinks that 1-800-Flowers.com is just the phone number and the Web site," she repeated unhesitatingly. Chris replied, "I share your frustration, and we need to address that." He said he was going to have Sheryl work with some of the company's best local marketing executives to come up with a plan to get people into her store. "Customers need to see what a great florist you are." Sheryl choked up, thrilled at the offer of help and overwhelmed by the vote of confidence.

Jose, confused at being brought to headquarters, cracked a wide grin when he recognized the man who walked through the door. His smile grew from ear to ear when he learned the true identity of his trainee. Explaining that he'd been looking to find the company's next generation of leaders, Chris said he'd found one in Jose. "We have a mentorship program, and I would be privileged and honored if you'd allow me to be your mentor. I'm pretty confident that if you and I work together, you could become the youngest franchise owner in the history of the company." Before Jose could respond, Chris continued, "To buy one of our franchises requires some money. But when you're qualified and ready to start, you can count on the first $25,000 coming from me." Grasping for words and overcome with emotion, Jose could only say it was the biggest thing that had every happened to him. His first order of business was a call to his mother to let her know the amazing news. "That was *Jim McCann's brother,* Mom. He's going to be my mentor. We're going to open a franchise." Even in the eyes of his new mentee, Chris was still Jim's little brother.

It was in that familiar role that Chris took to the stage of a flower-filled auditorium where the headquarters staff had been gathered. Revealing what he'd been up to for the past week, Chris shared video highlights of his misadventures. As he comfortably laughed along with the crowd and engaged in easy banter with individual colleagues, a transformation began to take place. The man who'd been in the wings for so long was now center stage, and not only was he shining in his new role, but the audience was readily accepting the metamorphosis. When the video finished, Chris turned serious, sharing what he thought was the core business lesson he'd learned from his experience: "There are things we're doing well, but there are also lots of details we need to pay more attention to. I'm lucky to be a boss of a company that's all about being thoughtful. I am making a commitment to each of you that from this day forward, *I* am going to be more thoughtful of *you*." It was obvious that the audience had also made a commitment, albeit unspoken—a commitment of support for the next leader of 1-800-Flowers.com.

As the crowd applauded appreciatively and Chris mixed with his undercover coworkers and their families, taking pictures and exchanging laughs, Jim McCann stood on the side taking it all in. His smile said he couldn't have been more impressed with Chris or prouder of him and the leadership and communication skills he'd displayed. Jim had always known that the future of the company was in good hands. Now, everyone else knew it as well.

Later, when the crowd had thinned out, Chris had a moment to reflect. "I realize now that going undercover wasn't really about proving to my brother, or anyone else, that I'm capable of leading this company. It was about proving to *myself* that I know what's necessary to lead this company into the future."

The little brother was ready to take the wheel.

SINCE THE SHOW

★ **Pauline's** dream has come true. She's been brought to the corporate headquarters to work on production and development strategies, and she's also been involved in two annual design council meetings. Last year, one of her designs was selected for inclusion in an upcoming collection. As a result of Chris's realization that florists were not being sufficiently informed about the company's opportunities for ongoing training, 1-800-Flowers.com launched a magazine called Florology, focusing on design and industry trends and providing information on training programs. Pauline has been the subject of a feature article.

★ **Sheryl** is working harder than ever since the local marketing team helped her get the word out about the store. Those outreach efforts, including offering floral arranging classes in the store, have boosted traffic dramatically. Appearing on national television didn't hurt either.

★ The incentive program inspired by **Nicole** was launched this past summer. Factory management is now actively seeking personal input from employees. Nicole's happy with the way management have taken her suggestions onboard.

★ The arrangement named after **Dee** is now officially part of the company's collection. Some of the proceeds are dedicated to a scholarship for aspiring floral designers. Dee jokes that she needs to be extra nice to all the new customers who've come in because they saw the show.

★ **Jose** is having monthly mentoring meetings with Chris. He's working on developing his selling skills, and plans to be the youngest franchisee in the company's history. Meanwhile, business at the store has picked up, with many people calling and asking to speak with him. He's sometimes recognized in the neighborhood, which makes him feel like a minor celebrity.

★ **Chris** is playing a visible role in the company, reaching out to make personal connections with employees, and encouraging all his managers to do the same. "We've always preached internally about the importance of having personal relationships with our customers. We have to do that with our employees as well." Although he doesn't think he'll be able to go undercover again, he has been encouraging other managers in the company to get out into the field. "I recently sent a number of our online team members out to visit actual florist shops, and they came back with all sorts of applicable insights." Despite the changing dynamics of their business relationship, Chris and his brother Jim are still teasing each other unmercifully.

GO UNDERCOVER IN YOUR OWN COMPANY

"I wish I could go undercover again. I'm giving advice to others in the company to find ways of doing it. I sent a number of our online team out to visit florist shops and they came back with all sorts of insights."

—Chris McCann, 1-800-Flowers

Every boss who went undercover returned convinced it was an incredibly valuable experience. Despite potentially embarrassing themselves in front of their boards, employees, and a few million strangers, they would all still recommend it to other business leaders and universally wished they could repeat the adventure. That's not because they're exhibitionists, but because no matter how hands-on as executives they were, no matter how much time they earnestly spent with frontline employees, they would always be treated as "the boss." The boss has the power to hire or fire, to promote or demote, to give a raise or pay cut. Why would anyone, from the new entry-level worker to the veteran manager, risk his or her livelihood to give the boss frank or even bad news? The only way to get past this barrier is to break ranks and pose as a new recruit. Even better, when you pose as a newbie, most people will instinctively take you under their wing and try to help you learn the ropes.

247

You don't need to be CEO or C-suite anything to go under-cover and learn how things really run every day. All you need is a sincere desire to know the real shape of things—and an organiza-tion big enough to allow you to slip in undetected. (More than one location is the key.)

If you are motivated to go undercover in your own organi-zation, your next question is likely where to start? How to pull it off? There is no blueprint—every boss on the show had his own unique experience and had to improvise a lot—but you can learn from their collective experience. . . .

1. Don't overdo the disguise. Because we're all busy and are bombarded by sights and sounds throughout the day, we take mental shortcuts. When we see someone in a suit and tie we think, executive. When we see someone in a uniform, baseball cap, or in casual, durable clothes, we think, frontline worker. Dress like you would on a casual Friday, or if you really were going to that job. Try too hard to dress in disguise, and you'll only stick out more. The more simple, the more likely you are to keep your identity secret. "All I did was take off my glasses and wear jeans and a baseball cap," recalled Churchill Downs's Bill Carstanjen. "Yet I walked by and even talked with people with whom I'd worked before and they didn't recognize me."

2. Plastic surgery isn't necessary. Your countenance might grace the pages of the company newsletter, but it's your "game face" the staff is used to seeing. Tweak your look just a bit and you won't be recognized. That means, if you're a man, letting your beard grow if you're usually clean shaven, or shaving if you usually have facial hair. If you don't wear glasses, put on a pair. And if you do, get contacts. A different hair cut would seal the deal, but isn't absolutely necessary. Cody Brooks of Hooters is a very public face of his company, on their posters and frequently in the media. Yet by shaving his goatee and adopting glasses, he sufficiently altered his image to appear as one more management trainee. On his return to headquarters, Coby endured some good natured ribbing from his executive team over losing his beard. "I would have shaved my whole head for the experience I went through," he offered, undeterred. "Going undercover helped me see that my problems aren't anywhere near as severe as those many people face. It was quite humbling. Since going undercover I find that I'm not dwelling as much on my own issues, and I'm trying to focus on others. I truly believe that if you take care of your people, and treat them well, your bottom line will work out."

3. Don't practice beforehand. While it might boost your ego to be instantly able to do the physical tasks you're assigned, it's not realistic. The average Joe coming in off the street won't have a chance to practice, so neither should you. No one expects an inexperienced newcomer to know the tricks of a job right away. If you do, you'll look like a ringer and raise alarm bells. Do your best and let your coworkers teach the ropes on the job. "Don't spend too much time worrying about whether you'll fail or be the source of jokes or laughter later on," suggested Rick Arquilla of Roto-Rooter. "In a strange way, you actually end up less vulnerable when you open yourself up to the possibility, even probability, of failing."

4. Don't dig for information. Resist the urge to play investigator and instead let the information emerge naturally. The average newcomer is too eager to get the job to risk ruffling feathers by pushing for dirt. Instead, ask natural, open-ended questions, like "is this a good place to work." The first impulse at most workplaces is to take pity on the new guy, so any widely held feelings about the job will emerge naturally—as long as you don't appear like a company spy. Waste Management's Larry O'Donnell was able to appear both eager and inexperienced, and so was able to get a great deal of insight from the unsolicited candid comments of a line leader at a recycling facility and a driver on a residential trash route. "The people doing frontline jobs at a company know quite a bit about how to make things better," offered Larry O'Donnell. "If you listen to them, and try to implement some of what they suggest, they will be so happy and engaged that it will make them feel even more a part of your team."

5. Don't offer suggestions. It's a fact of life in every workplace that suggestions aren't necessarily appreciated from the uninitiated. As a new hire, you won't change corporate mandates or processes on day 1 at a job. Pushing too hard will likely backfire, and cloud your own experience. Make a note of your idea, but don't broadcast it. See what you learn from others by experiencing the job from their vantage point. Michael Rubin of GSI Commerce noted, "The hardest thing about being undercover wasn't taking orders; it was seeing things that I didn't like, or that I thought could be done better, and not being able to address them."

6. Open up. The break room is the equivalent to the old-time neighborhood bar. People look for, and usually get, acceptance and support. Let people get to know you and show a genuine interest in getting to know them, too. "I was surprised by how open people were about their personal lives," admitted Joel Manby of Herschend Family Entertainment. "When you're an executive your meetings tend to be about particular problems and issues and there isn't a lot of time for personal interaction. I found it refreshing."

7. Arrive on time. When you're paid by salary and not by the hour, the exact time you arrive isn't a big deal. But when you have to clock in and out, when your pay is determined by the specific hours you work, an hour's pay makes a big difference in your life. Dave Rife of White Castle was made acutely aware that he'd shown up late for his first shift at the company's frozen food factory by his trainer for the day, and promised it wouldn't happen again. He has no qualms recommending the undercover experience to others. "Any executive who has a chance to go undercover in their organization shouldn't hesitate. If you go into it with an open mind and are willing to face the tougher side as well as the good side of it, you and your company can only grow and improve. On a personal level, the experience taught me to better open my eyes, my ears, and my heart and absorb everything I can from other people, no matter who they are or what their job or profession is."

8. Have fun with it. People go to work because they believe in what they do, and hopefully, they can believe in their bosses and their companies, too. Once you let go of control and fear of the unknown, you'll find it the most freeing experience. Ultimately, you'll realize why you love your job, and why you come in every day too. "When I first went undercover I thought I'd be focusing on finding areas to improve from an efficiency perspective," explained GSI Commerce's Michael Rubin. "I didn't realize I'd learn so much about the culture of the business and the people. I came away more energized than ever to create more opportunities for the great people who work for us." Joe DePinto of 7-Eleven agrees. "Every single employee

I met was amazing. What we have to do is support them better."
And Churchill Downs's Bill Carstanjen has this piece of advice:
"If you're going to go undercover you need to put aside your
own self-absorption and think about the people you're working
with. This experience is about them."

★ ACKNOWLEDGMENTS

There are many people who have contributed to the success of *Undercover Boss,* and we'd like to express our appreciation to all of them.

The show could only have happened because the leaders of some very substantial companies believed this was something worth doing, ignored the naysayers who said they were mad, cleared their diaries, and took the plunge. All the bosses in our first season were pioneers, but we're particularly grateful to Larry O'Donnell for having the courage to be the first in America and to Andy Edge for being the first in the United Kingdom.

The filming and editing of our programs wouldn't have been nearly as good without the wise words of advice, criticism, and encouragement we received from the network executives in CBS's reality department: Jen Bresnan and her two colleagues, Chris Castallo and Chris Carlson. The latter turned out to be so invested in the show that he subsequently resigned from CBS and joined us as the show runner for the second season. Many other people at CBS helped make the show a hit, particularly two members of Chris Ender's press and publicity team, Mitch Graham and Barbara Abseck, and Ron Scalera's marketing team. We were shocked to hear of Ron's sudden death just weeks after he'd so effectively overseen the high-profile launch of *Undercover Boss.*

The top brass at CBS demonstrated enormous faith in the appeal of our show by taking the extraordinary step of launching it immediately after the Super Bowl. It was a risk that could have gone sour very publicly, and we are most grateful to Kelly Kahl, Nancy Tellem, and, ultimately, Leslie Moonves. And the person who heard our pitch, was convinced by it, and championed our show throughout was Nina Tassler, to whom we owe a special debt.

In the United Kingdom, we're extremely grateful to Liam Humphries, Sue Murphy, and Julian Bellamy of Channel 4 for believing in our new start-up company and commissioning the show in its original paper form.

As executive producers, we are only as good as the many hardworking and talented people who actually produced the show on both sides of the Atlantic. In particular, we thank Stef Wagstaffe, Shauna Minoprio, and Jenny Crowther, our show runners in America and the United Kingdom. The first season was hard to cast, and Damon D'Amore, Beverley Self, and Michelle Mock were tireless in their approaches to so many companies. Bev and Andrew Pankin also helped in the preparation of this book, following up with all the bosses and the employees we featured. Jo Crawley, Amy Hussey, Andy Coker, and Nolan Ransdell oversaw production and finance; we hope they have some inkling of how grateful we are to them for everything they do to make our productions see the light of day and keep our company working so well.

Two other people who have made an enormous contribution to the success of our company are Jeanne Newman, our ever supportive and highly effective lawyer, and Greg Lipstone of ICM, the man behind so many reality show hits. Both of them were instrumental in ensuring that *Undercover Boss* made it to air and didn't bankrupt us in the process.

Finally, Stephen knows that the person who lies behind most of his successes is his wife, Jenni, and *Undercover Boss* was no exception. And Eli blames his loving mom, Sherry, and dad, John, for everything he does.

ABOUT THE AUTHORS

Stephen Lambert, chief executive of Studio Lambert, is one of Britain's best-known creative television executives, responsible for creating award-winning documentary format hits such as *Faking It, Secret Millionaire, Wife Swap,* and *Undercover Boss.* He started his career working for the BBC for 16 years making documentaries all over world, many in conflict areas such as Kuwait, Bosnia, Gaza, Iraq, South Africa, and Sri Lanka. He lives in London with his wife, Jenni Russell, a columnist for *The Guardian* and *Sunday Times*, and their two children.

Eli Holzman is president and cofounder of Studio Lambert USA, where he launched and executive produced *Undercover Boss.* He began his career at Miramax Films and founded Miramax Television, where he helped create *Project Greenlight* and the hit Bravo series *Project Runway.* For 20th Century Fox–based Katalyst Films, he developed and launched the CW series *Beauty & the Geek.* As an independent producer, his series creations include Bravo's *Work of Art.* He lives in Venice Beach, California.

Studio Lambert is a fast-growing independent production company based in London and Los Angeles. It creates and produces a wide range of nonfiction programs, especially documentary formats that it produces in both countries and licenses worldwide, such as *Undercover Boss, The Fairy Jobmother,* and *Three in a Bed.* Studio Lambert is part of the All3Media Group, one of the largest groups of television production companies in the world.

For more information on *Undercover Boss,* please visit www .cbs.com/undercoverboss.

⭐ PHOTO CREDITS

Sorting Through the Garbage
Waste Management: **Larry O'Donnell, President and COO**

p. 18   Formal headshot of Larry O'Donnell
                 by David Edmonson.

                 Undercover photo courtesy of Studio Lambert.

pp. 21, 35   Stills from the show provided by CBS.

Wings, Women, and Beer
Hooters of America: **Coby Brooks, President and CEO**

p. 44   Formal headshot of Coby Brooks
                 by Shane Durrance.

                 Undercover photo courtesy of Studio Lambert.

pp. 50, 54   Stills from the show provided by CBS.

The Necessities of Life
7-Eleven: **Joe DePinto, President and CEO**

p. 68   Formal headshot of Joe DePinto courtesy of
                 7-Eleven.

                 Undercover photo courtesy of Studio Lambert.

pp. 74, 76   Stills from the show courtesy of Studio Lambert.

An American Love Affair
White Castle: **Dave Rife, Owner**

p. 90   Formal headshot of Dave Rife by Jim Shively.

                 Undercover photo courtesy of Studio Lambert.

pp. 97, 102, 106 Stills from the show provided by CBS.

Time to Get Personal
Churchill Downs: Bill Carstanjen, COO

p. 116   Formal headshot of Bill Carstanjen
by Dan Dry and Associates.

                    Undercover photo courtesy of Studio Lambert.

pp. 124, 132, 134 Stills from the show courtesy of Studio Lambert.

Looking for Fulfilment
GSI Commerce: Michael Rubin, Founder and CEO

p. 142   Formal headshot of Michael Rubin courtesy of
GSI Commerce/TrueAction.

                    Undercover photo courtesy of Studio Lambert.

pp. 153, 157   Stills from the show courtesy of Studio Lambert.

What Riches Can't Buy
Herschend Family Entertainment:
Joel Manby, President and CEO

p. 168   Formal headshot of Joel Manby by Mike Williams.

                    Undercover photo courtesy of Studio Lambert.

pp. 179, 180, 185 Stills from the show courtesy of Studio Lambert.

Troubles Down the Drain
Roto-Rooter: Rick Arquilla, President and COO

p. 196   Formal headshot of Rick Arquilla by Jim Osborne.

                    Undercover photo courtesy of Studio Lambert.

pp. 202, 205, 207 Stills from the show courtesy of Studio Lambert.

Say It with Flowers
1-800-Flowers: Chris McCann, President and COO

p. 220   Formal headshot of Chris McCann courtesy of
1-800-Flowers.com.

                    Undercover photo courtesy of Studio Lambert.

pp. 230, 233   Stills from the show courtesy of Studio Lambert.